Construction Safety Management

Raymond Elliot Levitt

Associate Professor of Civil Engineering
Construction Engineering and Management Program
Stanford University

Nancy Morse Samelson

Construction Safety Management Consultant
Stanford, California

McGraw-Hill Book Company

New York   St. Louis   San Francisco   Auckland   Bogotá
Hamburg   Johannesburg   London   Madrid   Mexico
Milan   Montreal   New Delhi   Panama
Paris   São Paulo   Singapore
Sydney   Tokyo   Toronto

Library of Congress Cataloging-in-Publication Data

Levitt, Raymond E.
    Construction safety management.

    Bibliography: p.
    Includes index.
    1. Building—Safety measures.   I. Samelson,
Nancy Morse.   II. Title.
TH443.L48   1987   624'.028'9   86-27800
ISBN 0-07-037298-5

1234567890   DOC/DOC   893210987

ISBN 0-07-037298-5

The editors for this book were Nadine M. Post and Nancy Young,
the designer was Naomi Auerbach, and the production supervisor
was Annette Mayeski. It was set in Century Schoolbook by Byrd Press.

Printed and bound by R. R. Donnelley & Sons Company.

To the many foremen, superintendents, project managers, safety professionals, chief executives, and construction buyers, whose effective methods for improving construction safety we have described in this book, and to all those who share their concern for safety in the workplace.

Contents

Acknowledgments

This book is a compendium of the experience and knowledge of many more people in the construction industry than we can possibly list. To the extent to which this book helps the industry, these many contributors, mostly anonymous, deserve much of the credit. We have, therefore, dedicated the book to them.

We owe a special debt of gratitude to Professor Emeritus Clarkson H. Oglesby, who initiated the pioneering Construction Engineering and Management Program at Stanford University through which the research that forms the basis for this book was conducted. Professor Oglesby personally encouraged each of us, at different times, to join the program and to work on the problem of construction safety. He has continued to be a guide, a constructive critic, and a friend to each of us through the years since.

We also want to express our appreciation to another colleague and friend: Professor Emeritus Henry W. Parker for his years as principal investigator for the OSHA New Directions Grant through which many of the practical applications of the research were developed, for his work as thesis advisor for research studies in construction safety management, and for his coauthorship with us of the study on the user's role in improving construction safety performance.

Other colleagues in the Construction Engineering and Management Program, Professor John Fondahl, the program's director since 1974, and Professor Boyd C. Paulson, Jr., have been frequent sources of encouragement and support.

The members of the Executive Committee of the Construction Safety and Health Program gave freely of their time and their helpful advice through the years: John T. Banister, Joseph A. Barton, Richard Blach, Barbara Cohrssen, Dr. Alain Decleve, Harry Eckstein, Robert Gilmore, Marsha Grueber, Randolph Harris, Gerold C. Heiken, Paul Henson, Ed Maher, Dale Marr, Jerry Martin, Patty McFarland, Fred Ottoboni, Russell Peck, William Penrose, Frederick L. Peregoy, Anthony Ramos, Jack Short, Jack Sidlow, Mary-Lou Smith, Chester Stanaro, Robert J. Wetherall, and Walter Willard.

Others who contributed substantially include Warren Anderson, Robert E. Atkinson, Donald Barrie, James W. Beckett, Gaylord Blue, Tim Blue, Roger A. Brooks, Ron Bruce, Ron L. Brunner, William L. Burdick, Alan N. Campbell, Faye Chapman, Carroll Dunn, Don Eberts, Del F. English, Dorothy Erickson, Claire Fields, Diana Forsythe, Walter B. Garyotis, Margaret Gelatt, William Geraghty, Robert S. Gosnell, George Harris, Gregory Howell, Glenn L. Katz, Sharon Knecht, Rita Kuhn, Jim E. Lapping, Herman D. Little, Dewey Long, Lester N. Longbrook, Petrina Mao, James G. March, Donald Marquis, Jane Martin, C. Russell Matson, Tom K. McManus, Jr., Ruth Mota, Thomas G. Noel, Homer Olsen, Ian Paterson, J. O. Patterson, Douglas Ridgeway, Kenneth Sletten, Ben Stetson, R. Steven Ray, Dawnie Stephenson, Margaret Thompson, Roland Tripp, Malcoln Watson, Howard L. Wenrick, Christine Williams, Kay Weiss, Robert L. Wooten, and Ingo Zeise.

A number of graduate students conducted parts of the safety research reported here and have since become colleagues in industry or academia. Four have written Stanford Construction Institute technical reports: Lance William deStwolinski, who did the first safety research studies in the program in 1969; Jimmie Hinze, who researched the role of middle management; Michal Roger Robinson, who developed the accident cost accounting system; and most recently James Edward Koch, who investigated liability. Several coauthored technical reports with us: Jean Bretxa, Greg Mummy, and Lloyd Waugh on the evaluation of the line foreman training course and Dan Murphy on the follow-up study of the accident cost accounting system. Others who contributed to the research include: John Borcherding, Michael Fletcher, Edward Henderson, Michael London, Vaughn Prost, Michael Roarty, Dexter Salna, Kwaku Tenah, and Ignacio Umana.

During the years of the Stanford Construction Safety and Health Program a number of graduate students developed applications for the research findings to help the construction industry improve safety: Jim Aldrich, Russell Barnes, Mark Budwig, Roy Buis, Ellis Cha, David Cates, Harold Chapman, Wendell Collins, Michael B. Dunne, Sally Douglas, Pierre Dufour, Richard Ellis, John Everett, Charles Feghali, Karl W. Helmhold, Eric Herbert, Timothy L. Horst, Mark Johnson, Jay Kushner, Eric Lamb, George Lenes, Pam Lettrich, Michael Lieberman, Bonnie Murdock, Brad Rinzler, Robert Romine, Greg Shill, Grant Stevens, Mark Supica, Suzan Swabacker, Kenneth Vandroff, and Kent Werle.

Financial support for the research and applications described in this book came first from the Construction Institute and later from several sources: a New Directions Grant from the Occupational Safety and Health Administration, the Business Roundtable, the Associated General Contractors of California, and the Laborer's-AGC Education and Training Fund. We gratefully acknowledge the support provided by these organizations.

We each want to express special gratitude to our respective spouses, Kathleen and Hans, for their patience and support during the 2 years of days, nights, and weekends that they encouraged us to devote to the preparation of this book.

To all of the many people who have helped make this book a reality, our very sincere thanks—we hope that the results adequately reflect your contributions.

Introduction

Purpose of the Book

The purpose of *Construction Safety Management* is two-fold:

- To show why safety management is a key part of effective construction management
- To provide construction managers at all levels with proven effective techniques for managing construction work safely.

The book is aimed at construction managers—CEOs, job-site managers, superintendents, and foremen—as well as at those working with construction managers: construction safety professionals, insurance loss control specialists, and managers in the facility engineering and construction divisions of companies that buy construction services.

The backbone of the book is some 15 years of research on construction safety carried out by the authors and their colleagues in the Construction Engineering and Management Program of Stanford University's Civil Engineering Department.

The book documents the enormous savings that can be achieved by effective safety management in construction, and it shows how successful companies, project managers, foremen, and construction buyers have succeeded in making those savings. We detail the specific management methods found to be most effective for each participant in the construction process, and we provide real examples of companies putting these methods to work.

Scope and Limitations

Construction Safety Management deals with actions that managers at all levels can take to create an organizational setting in which workers will be trained and motivated to perform safe, productive construction work. Research indicates that over 80 percent of industrial accidents involve an unsafe act by a worker; therefore, we chose to address the behavioral rather than the physical side of construction safety in our research and in this book.

Those with the responsibility for managing safe construction and the safety professionals who support them will need to supplement the management principles presented here in two ways:

1. *With a thorough knowledge of the latest laws and standards for the various construction operations in the areas in which they are working.* For these extensive and constantly changing specifics, readers need to consult the applicable federal, state, and local safety regulations currently in effect for each project.

2. *With in-depth construction engineering knowledge of the many specific work methods required for ensuring safe construction operations.* For example, managers involved in underground utility construction need knowledge about different types of shoring and their suitability for the types of soil conditions in which they are working. Such details, not necessarily covered in regulatory safety standards, are of great importance in providing the highest levels of safety that can be engineered into a job. The engineering know-how for the tremendous variety of work operations involved in construction can be found in a variety of construction engineering handbooks, in trade association or other industry consensus documents, and in vendor reference manuals.

Our Philosophy

We examined the old myth that safety can only be achieved at the expense of costs and schedule. On the contrary, we found that the safest managers in many of the construction firms that we studied over the past 15 years turned out also to be the ones in their organizations with the best cost and schedule performance.

Moreover, we found that the construction managers at all levels whose subordinates have worked year in and year out with outstanding production and safety records—in some cases, for many years without a single lost-time injury—practice different management methods and techniques than their counterparts who have less impressive safety records. In the chapters that follow we have laid out the principles and methods used by these outstanding all around managers to deliver construction projects on time, under budget, and safely.

The Stanford Construction Safety Research Program

During the late 1960s Professor Clarkson H. Oglesby, leader of Stanford's Construction Engineering and Management Program, became convinced of the importance of involving researchers with formal training in the behavioral and social sciences in the program's ongoing construction research studies. Dr. Nancy Morse Samelson, one of the authors and a social psychologist by training, joined the group in 1971 as a research associate. With the passing of the Occupational Safety and Health Act (OSHA) in 1970, the industry's—and the Stanford Construction Program's—attention was focused on safety concerns. The Stanford group began a series of studies on behavioral aspects of construction safety, funded by the Stanford Construction Institute, that were designed to complement OSHA's focus on physical hazard elimination.

Professor Raymond Levitt, the other author, was a doctoral student who participated in the research program. His 1975 dissertation, *The Effect of Top Management on Safety in Construction*, was one of the first completed studies in this research program. Subsequent studies dealt with job-site managers and foremen. The most recent of the management studies, completed in 1981, dealt with the role of construction buyers.

Each of these studies compared the policies and practices employed by a representative sample of managers at that level, including some with outstanding safety records and others with average or poor safety performance. Using rigorous social science research techniques, each study separated out the management methods used by the safest practitioners and presented them in technical reports and articles.

Following upon these basic studies, we were funded by an OSHA New Directions Grant to conduct pilot safety improvement projects, e.g., with small roofing contractors, and to offer seminars and workshops to industry. We did this for 5 years, reaching several hundred firms with the results of our work.

Our study on the buyer's role in construction safety was funded by the Business Roundtable as part of its Construction Industry Cost Effectiveness (CICE) project. Over 100,000 copies of their summary report of our research have been distributed to construction buyers and contractors in the United States and elsewhere. As a result, many construction buyers have recently begun to prequalify or select contractors based, in part, on their safety performance.

Facing this increased interest in construction safety on the part of their clients, many contractors wanted to improve their firms' performance in this area and contacted us for reference materials. We found that the useful information for managers from Stanford's 15-year construction safety reseach program was scattered in numerous research reports, journal articles, and seminar materials. We determined that someone should compile the results of the research into a document that would be a comprehensive handbook on construction safety management. Hence this book.

A Note on the Organization and Style of the Book

We have attempted to present our research results in no-nonsense managerial language, interspersed with relevant examples drawn from our many interviews. Busy construction foremen, superintendents, project managers, and executives should be able to find the information they need from the book with a minimum of effort. References have been provided for readers who wish to consult the underlying research reports, but we have kept footnotes and appendices to a minimum. Our aim is to communicate valuable knowledge gleaned from the collective experience of hundreds of successful construction managers to the reader in the most effective way possible.

To make this book as readable as possible by its intended audience, we have followed the style of several popular books dealing with management. We have grouped a series of relatively short chapters of related material for each level of management into 6 separate sections of the book. Discussions of research methodology are very brief. Each section presents suggested safety management practices, examples of how successful companies employ them, and a summary of important action steps at the end.

One of the style issues which we had to face was the use of sex-neutral terminology. We struggled to find suitable words to describe each level of management neutrally and have tried to eliminate gender-specific pronouns wherever possible.

Our decision was to stick with widely used words such as foreman in the interest of clarity. We applaud the growing numbers of women who are becoming journeymen and foremen in construction and hope that new titles for these positions will evolve over time as their numbers increase.

In the many examples we have used to illustrate ideas presented in the chapters we have changed the names of companies and of individuals to preserve their anonymity. However, every one of these examples describes a real situation in one of the companies that we studied. We have, therefore, decided to use the pronouns "he" and "she" where they refer to these real—albeit anonymous—people in our examples.

A Reader's Guide

All readers of *Construction Safety Management* are encouraged to read Part 1 of the book, which documents the direct and hidden costs of construction accidents.

Chief executives of construction firms and senior managers (those with multiproject line responsibility) should also read Part 2 and the summaries at the ends of Parts 3, 4, 5, and 6.

Job-site managers should also read Part 3 and should review the summaries at the ends of Parts 2, 4, and 5.

Foremen and general foremen should also read Part 4, and the summaries at the ends of Parts 2, 3, and 5.

Construction safety professionals should also read Parts 5 and 6 especially carefully and should review Parts 2, 3, and 4 to know the guidelines for safety management at all levels.

Construction buyers should read Part 6 and should review the summaries at the ends of Parts 2, 3, 4, and 5.

The Bottom Line

Throughout the book we have taken the point of view that safety is an important dimension of organizational performance and one that managers can control in the same way that they can control cost and schedule performance. Moreover, our research has found that there is no trade-off between safety performance and performance in terms of cost or schedule. Rather safety, cost, and schedule are mutually reinforcing.

For this reason, organizations that succeed in improving their construction safety performance will see the results—amplified—in their organization's overall bottom-line performance.

Read on for details.

How Safety Saves Money

When Joe Reinhardt (not his real name), president of a small specialty construction company, told us that a carpenter had been badly hurt on one of his jobs and was in the hospital, he was obviously deeply disturbed.

Then we went out on Joe's jobs. There was no sign of his concern. Stairwells were not adequately guarded. Scaffolds were not well secured. Every job was full of accidents waiting to happen.

Why this inconsistency?

Talking with Joe we discovered a basic reason. He was sad that a long-time friend had been in a serious accident, but he did not feel at all responsible for what had happened. He felt that construction was a dangerous business and nothing could be done to change that.

The word is now spreading that many construction contractors, job-site managers, and foremen have proved that management efforts can result in reducing accidents. The belief in the inevitability of construction accidents is gradually disappearing, but it was widespread. One safety professional, recalling the old days, says:

In the early years of building construction, it was common practice to assume that accidents would claim one life for each two floors of a building or for each million dollars of general construction work performed or for each half-mile of tunnel construction. At that time, these numbers were actually put in the job estimate.

In those early days there must have been many contractors who felt that there was nothing to be done to change this situation. Now we have learned from construction managers what they do to keep accidents from happening. This book describes in detail the methods used by company presidents, job-site managers, and foremen who have outstanding safety records. These methods can be adopted by any construction president, job-site manager, or foremen and will lead to substantial improvements in their safety records. But, to be the devil's advocate, why should anyone change?

For some contractors the pain and suffering to workers and their families that result from construction injuries and deaths are strong enough reasons by themselves for requiring effective safety management on their jobs. But for many contractors the humanitarian reasons cannot stand alone. They feel that no matter how good an idea working safely is, it has to be cost effective. In this section we shall take a close look at the economic facts. They clearly demonstrate that safety management pays off handsomely in financial as well as humanitarian terms.

The reason why effective safety management is a profit maker for construction companies is that **accidents have high direct and indirect costs, and management can control these costs.**

The **direct** *costs are insured. These include medical costs and other workers' compensation insurance benefits as well as liability and property-damage insurance. Of these, claims under workers' compensation, the insurance that covers workers injured on the job, is the most substantial of the direct costs.*

For most construction companies these direct costs of accidents are not fixed. They vary depending upon each company's own accident experience. In order to show how this works, we will describe the workers' compensation insurance system and the experience modification rating (EMR) in Chapter 1.

Indirect *(noninsured) or hidden costs are the other—and much larger—part of the economic burden imposed by a poor accident record. Reduced productivity, job schedule delays, added administrative time, damage to equipment and facilities, and the costs of administering and handling workers' compensation insurance are some of the many types of hidden costs associated with accidents. We will document these hidden costs in detail in Chapter 2.*

If the bill is so expensive—and we will demonstrate in

detail that it is—*why have many contractors failed to notice this substantial cost drain?*

The main problem has been that the methods of cost accounting typically used by construction firms for keeping track of project costs bury accident costs.

The direct costs of past accidents, including medical bills and workers' compensation benefits, are frequently combined with other insurance costs as part of the overall figure for labor burden. Moreover, these are not the current costs from accidents on each particular project. Rather the current bills for accident costs on each project go to the insurance company and keep coming in long after the project is over.

The indirect costs of project accidents are equally difficult to discover from project financial statements. They are hidden in extra labor, material, and equipment costs which result from—but are never attributed to — accidents.

Although the costs of accidents are not highlighted by typical cost accounting systems, we will show that they can come back to haunt a company in subsequent years through increased workers' compensation premiums. For construction companies with very poor safety records, these increased insurance premiums can be costly enough to render a company noncompetitive against safer firms.

A central theme of this book is that the direct and indirect costs of accidents are no different from any other cost of doing business. They can be contained by appropriate management techniques. Once senior managers in a construction company become aware of the magnitude of these costs and realize that they can be reduced to near zero by aggressive safety management, the company is on the way to improving its safety performance.

The purpose of the first part of the book is to set out the cold hard facts which prove that accidents are a heavy financial burden on construction firms. The remainder of the book describes successful construction management techniques for reducing accidents and their costs.

1

The Biggest Single Cost Saving

As we began to work with construction companies to help them improve their safety performance, we found that there were some major misconceptions. Contractors often showed little initial interest in their workers' compensation insurance, saying that they paid their broker to take care of it for them.

We noted that they knew their other expenses down to the last penny, yet here was an expense of thousands of dollars a year (an amount that often exceeded total profits for a company) which they knew little about. Their reason was that they believed that the rates for workers' compensation were fixed, so there was little they could do about these costs.

Here was the crux of the problem. *Workers' compensation insurance is not like fire insurance.* They did not realize that they were bearing the brunt of their own accident experience. Furthermore competitors who had few accidents would be paying significantly lower costs for workers' compensation.

Contractors who have a good grasp of workers' compensation insurance and know how these costs are calculated are on the way to improving their profits.

Prior to workers' compensation insurance laws, injured workers were required to prove that the employer was responsible for the worker being injured in order to receive any compensation for injuries received on the job. Workers' compensation insurance was developed to provide a no-fault plan for dealing with industrial injuries.

Under the workers' compensation insurance laws, workers injured on the job forfeit the right to sue their employers for the costs of injuries. In return, they gain paid medical treatment and compensation for the time off from work through insurance provided by their employers.

The state legislators who developed the workers' compensation laws wanted to include an economic incentive for employers to improve safety on their jobs. They realized that if each employer doing a certain type of work had to pay the same amount—an average of all the accident costs in that type of work—there would be no incentive. Employers with good accident records would be penalized since they paid much more of the costs than they had incurred, while the employers with the poor accident records would be rewarded because they paid much less of the costs than they had incurred.

The cost of workers' compensation insurance has, therefore, two components. The first component, the "manual rate," is based on the average of medical costs and benefits paid out in the previous year for each type of work. The second component, the "experience modification rating" (EMR), is based on each employer's accident costs compared to the average.

Manual Rates

Unless contractors are self-insured or covered by insurance carried by their client, they must buy insurance to cover their workers' compensation exposure. The cost of this insurance varies, as workers' compensation insurance is controlled by each individual state legislature and accident claims are settled in accordance with state law.

The manual rates are calculated by states annually for about 450 work classifications (e.g., plumbing, reinforcing steel installation) based on the medical costs and benefits paid for accidents in each particular work classification plus an amount to cover administrative costs and profits of the insurance company and administrative costs for the rating bureau. Each year's rates reflect the costs for the previous year and are expressed in dollars per $100 dollars of payroll. Therefore a look at the manual rates shows the comparative accident costs of different trades within construction. As an example, the typical rate for structural ironworkers is about 4 times that for electricians.

Since these rates are published by the rating bureaus in manuals or books, these average workers' compensation rates have come to be called "manual" or "book rates."

The mix of types of work in which a contractor is engaged and the proportion of total payroll for each work classification, then, will determine the *manual rate* for a contractor. It is important to realize that all contractors with that particular mix of work and size of payroll have the same manual rates. The workers' compensation laws assign to the rating bureaus the task of calculating these average costs yearly. Insurance carriers have no part in this process beyond supplying the claims data.

Calculating the Manual Rate

To show how these costs are calculated, we will follow through an example for a large project with a $30 million payroll, using the mix of trades for a typical large industrial project (Levitt et al., 1981, 1985). The calculation of the manual rates is illustrated in Table 1.1.

A contractor working in the state of California with the payrolls in the work classifications described in Table 1.1, whose rates were based on the California 1983 rates, would have a manual insurance cost of $2,374,380.

If there were no second component to calculating workers' compensation, this type of insurance would be like fire insurance. All contractors with the same payrolls in the work classifications would be paying the same amount, regardless of their accident experience. Instead, each eligible employer's claims experience *modifies* the average costs.

TABLE 1.1   Typical Workers' Compensation (WC) Premium Rates for a $100 Million Industrial Construction Project

Classification	Payroll[1]	WC rate[2]	Insurance cost
Pipefitters	$ 9,900,000	5.57	$ 551,430
Electricians	4,500,000	4.36	196,200
Laborers	5,400,000	9.85	531,900
Ironworkers			
Structural	1,800,000	16.17	291,060
Rodmen	1,800,000	7.68	138,240
Carpenters	2,700,000	9.98	269,460
Millwrights	1,500,000	10.17	152,550
Crane operators	1,200,000	11.85	142,200
Masons	600,000	8.27	49,620
Painters	600,000	8.62	51,720
Total	$30,000,000		$2,374,380

[1] Base salary, excluding overtime premiums and fringe benefits.
[2] $ per $100 of insured payroll, using the California 1983 rates.
SOURCE: Samelson & Mauro (1983) adapted from Levitt et al. (1981).

The Experience Modification Rating

The purpose of the experience modification rating is that contractors who have experienced more accidents and higher claims costs than the average pay a surcharge, while those with lower than average claims costs receive a discount. [The only employers not eligible for experience rating are those with very few employees. For example in California after January 1, 1986, any employer with $13,100 or more in premiums (based on manual rates) would be eligible for experience rating.]

The rating bureaus calculate each eligible employer's experience modification rating. Four states have their own rating organizations: California, Delaware, New Jersey, and Pennsylvania. Six states have funds set up by the state to pay workers' compensation claims. Called "Monopolistic State Funds" and administered by a state board, these occur in Nevada, North Dakota, Ohio, Washington, West Virginia, and Wyoming. These six states use different methods for calculating the experience rating, ranging from systems very similar to the intrastate ratings to those giving little credit for better safety records. The remaining 40 states use the National Council on Compensation Insurance as their rating organization.

There are therefore two classifications of experience modification rating: the interstate EMR and the intrastate EMR. The interstate EMR is based on the accident claims experience of a contractor in any or all of the 40 states using that service. The intrastate EMR is based on a contractor's claims experience in the one state giving the rating.

The insurance carriers have no role in calculating these experience modification rates; they only provide the data on premiums and losses to the appropriate rating bureau for each contractor they insure. Therefore the carriers cannot compete by varying the insurance rates they charge and the resulting workers' compensation premiums.

The competition among insurance companies thus revolves around the method and time of payment, the types and extent of services offered, and the amount of money the insurance company retains for unsettled claims, as well as the rates charged for builder's risk and liability insurance which are often sold as a package with workers' compensation insurance.

How is an experience modification rating calculated? The number of components in the formula make the actual calculation complex. The following comments of one contractor are echoed by many more:

> I defy the layman, or almost anybody who is not in the insurance industry, to calculate a company's experience modification rating and determine if the rating is correct and doing what it's intended to do.

The complexity of these calculations is one reason why the EMR's original purpose, motivating employers to improve their safety performance, has been almost completely lost. The EMR has become the province of insurance experts, a mysterious set of figures which somehow affects the cost of workers' compensation insurance.

Granted that the details of the formula are complicated, the basic meaning of the experience modification rating is not. The experience modification rating is a modifier of the average premium cost (or manual rate) based on a contractor's own past accident claims experience.

An EMR of 60 percent means that the contractor pays a workers' compensation premium which is 60 percent of the manual rate premium because of a better-than-average claims experience. An EMR of 110 percent, on the other hand, means that the firm had higher claims costs than the average firm in its type of work classifications and will be paying 110 percent, a surcharge of 10 percent over the manual rate.

EMRs and Premium Costs

Surveys conducted for the study of the owner's role in construction safety (Levitt et al., 1981, 1985) showed that contractor's EMRs range very widely. In a sample of national industrial contractors, interstate experience modification ratings ranged from 50 to 205 percent, while the range for contractors with California EMRs was even greater: 35 to 260 percent. Some contractors, therefore, are paying 4 to 7 times as much for their workers' compensation coverage as their safety-aware competitors. How strong the impact of EMRs can be on premium costs is illustrated in Table 1.2, in which the manual rates and work classification mix described in Table 1.1 were used.

The meaning of this table can be spelled out in more detail by relating the costs of workers' compensation insurance for contractors to their direct labor payroll.

TABLE 1.2 EMR Impact on Cost of Worker's Compensation Insurance for Typical $100 Million Industrial Construction Project

EMR	Cost of WC insurance
35	$ 831,033
50	1,187,190
60	1,424,628
100	2,374,380
140	3,324,132
260	6,173,388

TABLE 1.3   Cost of Workers' Compensation for "Typical" Construction Projects (per $100 Million of Project Cost, Using 1981 California Manual Rates)

Type of facility	Experience Modification Ratings		
	EMR of 50	EMR of 100	EMR of 140
Paint plant	$ 380,000	$ 760,000	$1,064,000
Paper mill	417,500	835,000	1,169,000
Chemical plant	460,000	920,000	1,288,000
Power plants			
Coal	1,050,000	2,100,000	2,940,000
Nuclear	1,080,000	2,160,000	3,024,000

SOURCE: Adapted from Levitt et al. (1981, 1985).

If we assume that direct labor is 25 percent of the project cost, it can be shown from this table that the cost of workers' compensation insurance for a contractor with an EMR of 50 would be 4.7 percent of direct labor payroll.

$$\frac{\$1,187,190}{\$100 \text{ million} \times 25\%} = 4.7\%$$

The cost of workers' compensation insurance for a contractor with an EMR of 140 would be 13.3 percent of direct labor payroll.

$$\frac{\$3,324,132}{\$100 \text{ million} \times 25\%} = 13.3\%$$

The cost of workers' compensation insurance for a contractor with an EMR of 100, i.e., at the manual rate, would be 9.5 percent of direct labor payroll.

$$\frac{\$2,374,380}{\$100 \text{ million} \times 25\%} = 9.5\%$$

The difference in workers' compensation insurance costs in this example between a contractor with an EMR of 50 and one with an EMR of 140 is over $2 million, more than 8 percent of direct labor payroll.

Different types of construction projects show contrasting average costs for workers' compensation, as well as different ranges of costs for EMRs at 50 and 140. These contrasts are illustrated in Table 1.3.

Comparing these different types of construction projects brings out two related points: (1) the workers' compensation costs are much higher for some types of construction than others; (2) therefore, there is also a greater possibility for savings through reducing EMRs in some types of construction than others.

The higher costs of workers' compensation insurance for some types of projects result from differences in the mix of trades. Those types of construction with larger payrolls of workers in trades with high levels of accidents will have higher average workers' compensation costs.

Another contributing factor to differences in workers' compensation costs can be the fact that labor is a larger percentage of project costs for some types of construction than others. Building nuclear plants, for example, is both more labor intensive and employs many more workers in high-accident work classifications than building paint plants.

Table 1.3 also shows that the difference between a contractor with an EMR of 50 and one with an EMR of 140 ranges from 0.7 percent of project costs for paint plant contractors to 1.9 percent for nuclear power plant contractors.

Paint plant

$$\frac{\$1,064,000 - 380,000}{\$100 \text{ million}} = 0.68\%$$

Nuclear power plant

$$\frac{\$3,024,000 - 1,080,000}{\$100 \text{ million}} = 1.94\%$$

Contractors who reduce their EMRs can save sizable amounts of money. Spending time to understand the general way that EMRs are calculated is therefore worthwhile.

Calculating an EMR

The actual formula for calculating an EMR is not as important as understanding the elements which are included in the formula and how they can affect a contractor's EMR.

The experience modification rating is a modifier based on a *company's past accident experience as reflected in insurance records at the time that the report is sent to the rating bureau.* It is used in calculating a company's workers' compensation insurance premium.

Each part of that definition is important. The first element then is: What is meant by "past" accident experience? The time period used in the EMR calculations for a given year is the 3 years prior to the immediate past year. (This last year of claims is not used because there may be a number of accidents for which some of the costs are not in.)

Because of this time lag and the combining of data from 3 years, a firm which shows a year's improved safety performance has to wait 2 years before its better safety record has any effect at all on the EMR and thus on the insurance premiums. Even then the new better record will be weighed down by the 2 earlier years of poorer accident experience.

This system of basing each company's EMR for any given year on 3 past years of accident experience 1 year removed is designed to smooth out extreme fluctuations in insurance costs. However, since it also makes the connection between a company's accident experience on particular projects and the related insurance costs indirect, it weakens the immediate motivational effect. Improving a company's EMR thus takes a commitment over a number of years.

The next element of the EMR calculations is the definition of "accident experience." The formula includes both frequency and severity of accidents, *but it counts frequency much more heavily*. Thus if a company had one very severe accident during the year with claims adding to $30,000 and a competitor with the same payroll in the same work classifications had 15 accidents with claims of $2000 each during the same year, the competitor's EMR would be considerably higher. *Frequency of accidents is penalized in the EMR calculations*. The reasoning behind this is that it was considered that frequency of accidents was more controllable than severity.

The third element of the formula is: "as reflected in insurance records at the time that the report is sent to the rating bureau." Accident claims costs have two stages: (1) the insurance company is notified of the accident and puts into the company's accident cost records *a reserve* to cover the coming bills from that accident and (2) the reserves are removed from the company's accident cost record when all bills are paid.

The problem comes in the timing of the report sent to the rating bureau. Each carrier has to send what is called a "unit statistical report" to the rating bureau. Since these reports have to be sent to the rating bureau 6 months prior to the starting date of the next year's EMR, the insurance company may be maintaining reserves for a number of accidents. *These reserves are included in that year's accident costs for calculating the company's EMR even though they are conservative predictive costs rather than actual costs*. This method of handling unclosed claims accounts means that two contractors with the same accident frequency and severity profiles and the same accident claims costs may still have different EMRs. There are two ways that this result can come about:

1. Through differences in reserving policy among insurance companies. The contractor who has chosen an insurance company with a

much more conservative reserving policy will have the higher EMR and will be consistently paying higher insurance premiums.

2. Through differences in monitoring insurance reserves among contractors or their brokers. Contractors who are watching their accident statements from the insurance company very closely to be sure that reserves are no longer maintained when the claims are over or who negotiate down the size of reserves prior to the statistical report date will have lower EMRs than those who do not monitor their reserves.

Often companies have separate departments which handle insurance and safety, with little communication between the two. However, with the growing awareness of the importance of managing insurance, more and more contractors are developing new staff jobs which combine responsibility for monitoring both safety performance on the job and workers' compensation insurance costs.

A contractor we know with a very well-developed safety program is also very aware that insurance reserving practices can reduce the extent to which an excellent safety record translates into a very low EMR. He has assigned this insurance-reserve-monitoring function to a safety engineer who keeps very close tabs on who is off work and when they come back and lets the insurance company know immediately when the worker is back on the job.

The removal of the reserves before the end of the rating period can make a substantial difference in a company's EMR. Reviewing claims prior to the statistical report date will mean that only current reserve figures are used in the EMR calculations. Major claims should be reviewed at least every 6 months with the reviews scheduled so that corrected reserves will be reflected in the unit statistical report for the coming year.

Contractors who will be bidding long-term projects may want to estimate what their next year's EMR will be. This can be done using the information in the unit statistical report plus the last premium audits.

Understanding the relationship between EMR and insurance costs can also help the contractor avoid the pitfall of consistently classifying borderline work into the work classification with the lower manual rate. Two of the companies interviewed in the top management study lost money through this mistake (Levitt, 1975).

Knowing the manual rates, these contractors assumed that classifying a borderline type of work in a less hazardous category would save them money because they would then pay a lower manual rate. The problem came in the next part of the calculations, when their experience modification rating was used to modify the average premium. Since they classified the work as less hazardous than it was, their claims experience turned out to be less favorable than that of the average contractor in that classification. They thus had higher EMRs which resulted in higher future premium costs. These increases in premiums were in effect for several years and more than offset the up front savings in premiums.

The goal of keeping a low experience modification rating has taken on added importance to contractors since owners have begun to ask for EMRs as one means of gauging a construction company's safety record and as an indicator of a contractor's comparative insurance costs for accidents. This use of the EMR in selecting or prequalifying contractors will be discussed in more detail in Chapter 25.

Alternative Plans for Workers' Compensation

Contractors have decisions to make on methods of paying for workers' compensation. Among the options to be considered are full or partial self-insurance, retrospective rating plans, and dividend plans.

Full or partial self-insurance

Some firms are large enough that they choose to self-insure for workers' compensation. Financial and other requirements for demonstrating responsibility and capacity to self-insure vary from state to state. In effect, the firm pays its premiums into an escrow account and either staffs up to administer claims or, more commonly, contracts with an outside firm for claims handling and administration. We have found that firms that are able to meet the requirements for self-insurance become very safety conscious, since they now participate directly in the benefits (or losses) of their safety performance. We recommend that eligible contractors become fully self-insured.

Firms that are unable to meet the requirements for full self-insurance may still qualify for partial self-insurance. Under partial self-insurance, a firm would pay reduced premiums and might be responsible for, say, the first $1000 of accident costs for each employee, up to a maximum of $5000 total per accident. This alternative is similar to accepting a deductible in exchange for lower premiums under a private automobile policy. We recommend that firms which cannot meet the requirements for full self-insurance consider this option. It can free up premium dollars until the time that benefits are paid, and it can serve to heighten awareness of accident costs among senior management and throughout the firm.

Dividend plans

Many insurance carriers offer dividend plans. Under these plans, firms can be eligible to receive a dividend at the end of the current year if their actual losses (including any reserves for open cases) are below expected losses, based upon the premiums paid by the firm during the year. Insurance carriers do not guarantee these dividends; if the carrier has a bad year, it may not pay them. In practice, however, most carriers do pay dividends to eligible clients in all but very bad years.

Construction firms should be aware of what we call the "Santa Claus" effect of dividend plans. The method of payment makes construction companies feel that they are saving a great deal of money when they may not be. The more premiums a firm has paid up front, the easier it is to earn a dividend. Moreover, the dividend check is highly visible whereas the original premium payments were made routinely by the firm's accounting department each pay period. Consequently, such dividend plans can produce the Santa Claus effect since the dividend check coming at the end of the year (Christmastime) can make management feel that their safety record is saving the firm money when the opposite may well be true.

Remember that a low experience modification rating is the way to save money on workers' compensation insurance, and it is a good indicator of safety performance; a big dividend at the end of the year is not. As explained in the top management study (Levitt, 1975), a firm could earn dividends 2 years out of every 3 without ever lowering its experience modification rating. The dividend in such cases is simply the repayment of your interest-free loan to the insurance carrier rather than an indication of a long-term reduction in insurance costs. It is therefore necessary to look carefully at the original premiums over several years (which are a direct function of the EMR), rather than at the dividends in a given year, to discover whether or not the company is reducing accident costs.

Retrospective rating plans

A somewhat analogous alternative which is seldom used today is called retrospective rating. Companies with large enough accounts can elect to be retrospectively rated at the end of each year. Under this plan, the firm and its carrier negotiate a nominal premium to be paid up front, along with minimum and maximum levels of premium for the year. The actual premium to be paid is computed retrospectively at the end of the year, based upon the firm's experience during that year. Then an adjustment is made by a payment or credit, within the limits of the negotiated minimum and maximum premium amounts. The firm gains the advantage of paying lower premiums up front and the potential of further savings in return for accepting the risk that premiums may end up being higher (up to the negotiated maximum premium) than they would be using the EMR.

These alternative arrangements are attempts to design more attractive options for different types and sizes of firms that purchase workers' compensation insurance. Full or partial self-insurance and retrospective rating bring the firm closer to being self-insured than it is under the experience rating system alone. One alternative which takes a construction firm further away from being self-insured is wrap-up or owner-furnished insurance. This is discussed at length in Chapter 27.

We have seen in this chapter how, through its impact on the experience modification rating, safety management reduces construction costs by lowering the largest single cost of accidents: workers' compensation premiums. But improving job safety also cuts a host of hidden costs which can make the accident bill much higher than is usually realized. The nature and size of these hidden costs are worth examining by any cost-conscious contractor and are discussed in Chapter 2.

2

The Hidden Cost
of Accidents

Safety professionals are fond of drawing pyramids or icebergs to demonstrate the relation between the direct costs of accidents and the indirect costs. The top of the pyramid or iceberg represents the costs of workers' compensation insurance premiums. Down below is another group of costs presumed to be much larger. But these drawings of pyramids and icebergs have always prompted the questions in our mind: "How much larger are these hidden costs?" "Exactly what other costs are important ones?" No one seemed to have factual answers to these questions, so we gathered data on hidden costs as part of the study of the owner's role (Levitt et al., 1981, 1985).

Obviously obtaining information on hidden costs is not as easy as obtaining information on the medical costs and benefits under workers' compensation. The direct costs are available to contractors. Contractors only need to examine the records sent to them from their insurance company. The records of the indirect costs of accidents, however, are not routinely kept. And contractors are not accustomed to thinking about them. This explains, in part, why there was so little hard data.

Hidden costs of accidents are not only rarely recorded but also some of them are very hard to quantify. What kind of cost estimate, for example, should be put on adverse publicity to a company from an accident? How can one obtain solid dollars and cents figures on the long-range declines in the morale and productivity of workers after a number of serious accidents? These were tough questions to answer.

A Questionnaire on Hidden Costs

We decided to start with an easier job: to pinpoint the more easily measureable hidden costs. The following are the areas which we included in a questionnaire for contractors. The questionnaire asked contractors to list the costs of each of the following items for a number of individual accidents.

Transportation: Include the cost of emergency transportation (ambulance, taxi, pickup) at cost value, together with the cost of personnel that were necessary to get the injured worker to proper medical facilities.

Wages paid to injured worker for time not worked: Include all the time in which the worker was not actually doing his or her job and for which wages were paid. Consider time spent in the dispensary, the remainder of a day given off, etc.

Costs incurred because of delays which resulted from accident: Were other crews affected or delayed? Was equipment idled? Were tools that had an impact on the job lost or destroyed? Was the total duration of the project lengthened? Include all wages, rental fees, and indirect supervision costs that occurred as a result of the accident.

Costs of overtime necessitated by accident: Was overtime necessary to prevent project delay? Would it have been necessary had the accident not occurred? Calculate costs and include here.

Loss of efficiency of crew: Decreased crew efficiency can be the result of a morale problem or the reshuffling that might occur to replace an injured worker. Unless you have meticulous records, this quantity will have to be estimated. The best source of information would be the foreman or the supervisor.

Cost to break in and/or teach replacement worker: If a new worker was hired, include administrative expense in the hiring process. Include wages paid while in processing, training, and during orientation. Include also wages paid to the foreman or whoever is assigned to orient or train a new worker. If the new worker is less efficient than the replaced injured worker, quantify this loss of efficiency in terms of dollars and cents (i.e., if the foreman estimates the new worker is about 75 percent as efficient as the injured worker, then 25 percent of the worker's wages—over the entire period of less productive time—should be counted in this category).

Extra wage costs, slower returned worker: Frequently companies encourage a worker to return to the job site even though the person is partially and/or temporarily disabled. If this is so, the worker is probably working at a different, less demanding job or has returned to the former job at decreased efficiency. As in the previous question, quantify this decrease in productivity.

Costs for clean-up, repair or replacement, and stand-by costs: If the accident involved only an injury and had no other effects on the job, disregard this question. However, an accident frequently involves spillage, cave-ins, vehicle damage, material wastage, or site cleanup. Quantify these costs as closely as possible, either by calculating the wages necessary to correct the situation, the total cost of reconstructing damaged work, or from invoices received for repairs necessitated by the accident.

Costs to reschedule work: Include time spent by supervisors, engineers, and foremen to review schedules, and the resultant costs of adjusting to the new schedule.

Costs of wages for supervision as a result of the accident: Include all time spent on the accident and its results: caring for the worker's medical treatment, investigating the accident, completing forms, disseminating information, visiting the worker (if done while being paid), planning to prevent recurrence, appearance in court or meeting with investigators, etc.

Costs for safety and clerical personnel as a result of the accident: Typing, investigating, forwarding forms, time with press, etc.

OSHA and civil fines: Self-explanatory.

Cost of legal assistance: Include all out-of-pocket costs.

Other costs: Include, with an explanation, any other costs that were caused or were incurred because of the incident.

Questionnaire Results

Using this questionnaire on indirect costs, a group of safety-conscious companies gauged the level of these types of costs for 49 construction accidents which had occurred in their companies. Several interesting results came from this study:

1. The range of indirect costs for an accident was very great (from $221 to $30,627).

2. On the average hidden costs were almost 4 times the medical claims and insurance benefits paid to injured workers, but the ratio of indirect costs to direct costs varied widely.

3. Non-lost-time accidents, with their smaller insurance benefits, had proportionally larger hidden costs.

4. Every category of indirect cost showed a considerable range:
   a. Transportation: $17 to $500
   b. Worker's wages: $11 to $248
   c. Others' wages: $12 to $1120
   d. Overtime costs: $15 to $2930
   e. Efficiency loss: $10 to $6180
   f. Break-in replacement: $34 to $1125
   g. Slower returned worker: $80 to $7100
   h. Materials, equipment, cleanup, etc.: $3 to $3500
   i. Rescheduling costs: $11 to $600
   j. Supervisor costs: $10 to $600
   k. Clerical costs: $15 to $2000

Looking over these categories and ranges, we see that even this small sample of accidents from safety-conscious companies (which may be in a position to control hidden costs more effectively than less safe companies) shows some very high, easily measurable indirect costs for accidents. In fact adding up the high end of each category, the total indirect costs for a single accident could be $25,903.

Obviously there are many variables which can affect the amount of cost in a particular category:

- Transportation costs, for example, can be affected not only by severity of injury but by the closeness to necessary medical facilities.

- Cost incurred because of delays which resulted from an accident depend on the extent to which the accident affects the schedule and how critical the affected activities are to the project schedule at the time of the accident.

- Loss of efficiency of crew may depend on the type and severity of the accident and the feeling that the crew has toward the injured worker, and the extent to which the crew feels that the accident could have been prevented by management actions.

- The size of indirect costs from maintaining an injured worker on the job may depend on the extent to which the type of injury affects the worker's efficiency level and the initial skill and wage level of the worker.

- The extent of material, equipment and cleanup costs depends primarily on the degree of damage to materials, equipment, etc., in the accident and on the cost of replacement.

Because of these and many other variables involved in accidents, it is difficult to ascertain an average hidden cost for construction accidents.

The average ratio of indirect or hidden costs to direct costs of 4:1 found in the research gives us a conservative rule of thumb to use in estimating accident costs.

However, the results make it clear that there is no simple relationship between size of benefits and hidden costs.

Non-lost-time accidents generally have larger multipliers than lost-time accidents (see Table 2.1). The lost-time accidents, although they have a smaller multiplier, represent larger direct costs (medical and disability benefits); so the magnitude of the hidden costs is substantial anyhow.

For the sample of accidents studied the average ratio for non-lost-time accidents is 5.4, while the ratio for lost-time accidents is 2.4.

The average ratio for all the accidents in the sample is 3.8, that is hidden costs were about 4 times larger than direct costs. For a number of reasons this figure is probably an underestimation of what would be obtained from a more extensive study of hidden costs: difficult to measure variables, such as company reputation and image or employee morale, were not included; the companies sampled were safety conscious and may have been better able to control the indirect costs; the company personnel making the judgments were not used to consider-

TABLE 2.1   Analysis of Direct and Hidden Accident Costs

Range of benefits paid ($)	Number of cases	Average benefits paid (direct costs) ($)	Average hidden costs ($)	Average ratio-hidden cost to benefits paid
Nonlost time				
0 to 199	13	125	530	4.2
200 to 399	7	250	1,275	5.1
≥400	4	940	4,740	5.0
Lost time				
0 to 2,999	9	869	3,600	4.1
3,000 to 4,999	8	3,947	6,100	1.6
5,000 to 9,999	4	6,602	7,900	1.2
≥10,000	4	17,137	19,640	1.1

SOURCE: Levitt et al. (1981, 1985) p. 16.

ing and calculating such costs and thus may not have included all such costs.

Adding Up the Accident Costs

The total financial cost of accidents in construction begins to come into focus if we look at a series of figures developed as a part of the Business Roundtable Construction Industry Cost Effectiveness Project in 1979–1980:

1. Construction was estimated to be a *$300 billion* per year industry in the United States alone.
2. Builder's risk and liability insurance averaged about 1 percent of direct labor payroll.
3. Workers' compensation insurance averaged about 7 percent of direct labor payroll.
4. Direct labor payroll was estimated to be about 25 percent of total project cost.

Using these four figures, we can calculate the insurance cost to the construction industry:

$$25\% \times (1\% + 7\%) \times \$300 \text{ billion} = 2\% \times \$300 \text{ billion} = 6 \text{ billion}$$

This $6 billion represents the cost of insurance to the construction industry annually in 1980. It includes both the direct costs, i.e., the claims cost, and one type of indirect cost: the administrative costs and other nonclaims charges of the insurance industry. Since industry sources have estimated that administration and profit for the insurance carriers is 35 percent and the cost of claims is 65 percent, estimated claims costs total about $3.9 billion. Four times the claims costs would be $15.6 billion for the indirect costs of accidents. Adding the $3.9 billion of direct costs to the indirect costs makes a total of $19.5 billion annually which accidents cost the U.S. construction industry and, in turn, the buyers of construction, using figures from 1979–80.

This figure of $19.5 billion a year in accident costs is a very conservative figure. Since the time of the study in 1979–80, the cost of both workers' compensation insurance and liability insurance have increased substantially. Also the measurement of hidden costs in the study left out many hidden costs which were difficult to quantify, so that the estimate of the total hidden costs of accidents in construction annually is low.

Another way of calculating accident costs is to add up the average cost of accidents to contractors as expressed in percent of direct labor costs:

- Insurance costs average about 8 percent of direct labor costs (workers' compensation insurance, 7 percent; liability insurance, 1 percent).

- Accident claims costs are estimated as 65 percent of the insurance costs (the remaining 35 percent being administrative costs), i.e., 5.2 percent of direct labor costs (8 percent times 65).

- Hidden costs are about 4 times accident claims costs, i.e., 20.8 percent of direct labor costs (5.2 percent times 4).

- Average claims costs plus hidden costs are therefore 26 percent of direct labor costs (5.2 percent plus 20.8 percent).

An average contractor then pays 26 percent of direct labor costs for accidents.

These very high costs to construction companies are avoidable. Our data from managers at all levels in construction demonstrate that construction accidents and their costs are controllable through management methods. Putting these construction safety management methods into effect can reduce both insurance costs and the indirect costs of accidents.

Costs of a Safety Program

Accidents are controllable and the discussion of these costs alone indicates that substantial savings can be made by reducing accidents. But companies which have not yet invested much in a safety program or are considering upgrading their present safety program may still want to know the net savings after the costs of an effective safety program have been paid. We only know of two bits of relevant information: a small study of the cost of safety programs which was undertaken in connection with the Business Roundtable study on improving construction safety performance and an estimate which we calculated using data from the five companies described in Part 5, "The Safety Professional."

The small study in the Business Roundtable *Construction Industry Cost Effectiveness Project Report A-3* (1982) states:

> Insurance costs, costs of injuries, and the expense of liability suits are easily documented and rather readily available. The cost of establishing and administering a construction safety and health program is somewhat less tangible, but can be estimated with reasonable accuracy. Data collected from a significant sample of contractors working at various construction sites in 1980 indicate that the cost of administering a construction safety and health program usually amounts to about 2.5% of direct labor costs. These costs include:

- Salaries for safety, medical and clerical personnel
- Safety meetings
- Inspections of tools and equipment
- Orientation sessions
- Site inspections
- Personal protective equipment
- Health programs such as respirator-fit tests
- Miscellaneous supplies and equipment

This study's estimate of 2.5 percent of direct labor costs for a safety program, however, includes a number of items which are mandated by law such as toolbox meetings and personal protective equipment. The law-abiding contractor, therefore, would have to pay these costs in any case. Figuring the added costs of a safety program which goes beyond the nondiscretionary costs of meeting the legal requirements is not easy.

One way of estimating the cost of such safety programs is to find what proportion of a company's direct labor payroll is spent for the salaries of safety professionals. The idea here is that the major costs of an effective safety program are the salaries of the safety professionals. Using an average salary of $35,000 and an estimate of 25 percent of dollar volume as direct labor payroll, the minimum and maximum ratios of salaries of safety professionals to direct labor payroll for the five companies used as examples in Part 5 were .04 and .8 percent, respectively (the ratios for the three companies in between were: .07, .4, and .06 percent). The likely added cost of a safety program beyond what is legally required may, therefore, be closer to 1 percent or less of direct labor payroll rather than 2.5 percent.

Looking ahead to the coming chapters, a small company with a well-developed system for managerial accountability for safety costs, new worker and foreman orientation programs, and a high proportion of workers, foremen, and job-site managers who continue with the company from job to job may well need only the services of a part-time safety professional.

Savings from an Effective Safety Program

Whether we take the Business Roundtable estimate of 2.5 percent of direct labor costs or a lower figure which more accurately represents the costs beyond those required by law, a comparison of the costs of a safety program with the savings to be realized from instituting such a program show the substantial benefits of instituting a good safety program.

A safety program investment of 2.5 percent of direct labor costs *or less* if used as recommended in this book should decrease claims cost *by a minimum* of 25 percent. Let us now calculate the direct and indirect cost of accidents for a 25 percent improvement in claims costs:

- Insurance claims costs will be 3.9 percent of direct labor costs (5.2 percent times .75).
- Hidden costs will be 15.6 percent of direct labor costs (20.8 percent times .75).
- Claims costs plus hidden costs will be 19.5 percent of direct labor costs (3.9 percent plus 15.6 percent).

Recalling that the industry average cost of accidents was 26 percent, we can now calculate a conservative range of net savings to be expected from introducing a safety program modeled on the recommendations from this book:

- The total savings expected from reducing claims costs 25 percent will be 6.5 percent of direct labor costs (26 percent minus 19.5 percent).
- The conservative range of net savings to be expected from introducing an effective safety program is 4.0 percent of direct labor costs (6.5 percent minus 2.5 percent).

The balance of this book describes what we mean by an "effective safety program." It is based upon detailed research results on how top managers, project managers, foremen, and others effectively manage safety along with productivity.

At the center of all the management methods, however, is one important prerequisite which needs to be emphasized in this section: the establishment of a method or methods to make accident costs continually visible to construction managers.

The very first step in the process of controlling the high cost of accidents is to bring these costs out into the open on construction projects. A new and very effective method for making accident costs immediately visible on the job is the Stanford Accident Cost Accounting System. Since this system is an excellent way to make construction people aware of the costs of accidents, it is discussed next.

3

Putting Accident Costs Up Front

The difference between a good corporate safety department and a good safety record was brought home to us on a complicated highway and bridge construction job. With the company's safety director and the project director, we planned a field test for a projectwide safety management improvement program. We expected full cooperation from the field superintendent for the project, whom we shall call Mac. But Mac threw so many roadblocks in our way that we withdrew.

The question in our minds was: "Why had Mac been so unwilling to work with us?" The story soon came out. Mac was an old-time carpenter who came up through the ranks, a hard-bitten realist who prided himself on meeting his costs and schedules. From the company's point of view he was an outstanding superintendent with a long history of successes in finishing projects on time and under budget.

We persuaded the safety director to find out from the company insurance department how much Mac's projects had been costing the company in accidents in recent years. Next these costs were compared with the profits on his jobs.

When the figures were tallied up, it turned out that Mac had been losing money for the company, not making it.

Mac's story illustrates a strange paradox in the construction industry: A very cost-conscious industry is ignoring a major area of costs. We have already touched on the reasons in the previous chapters. These are:

1. The longer time frame of accident costs in relation to the usual time frame of a job or project
2. The usual accounting method for handling insurance costs as part of the labor burden

3. The traditional separation of insurance from safety in the management structure of companies

4. The fact that workers' compensation costs have risen dramatically in recent years and thus are much more sizeable than they used to be

In this chapter we will show how cost-conscious companies are now beginning to ensure that the "Macs" of the construction industry are being evaluated on accident costs along with other job costs.

Our emphasis will be on one system which has now been tested and found successful by a number of companies: the Stanford Accident Cost Accounting System. We will compare this system with other means of accomplishing the purpose of making accident costs a reality at the job or project level.

The Stanford Accident Cost Accounting System was developed by Michal Roger Robinson and is described in detail in *Accident Cost Accounting as a Means of Improving Construction Safety* (Robinson, 1979). Recently a follow-up study of 13 companies which have been using the Stanford Accident Cost Accounting System has been completed (Levitt et al., 1987). Both of these reports will be drawn on for this chapter.

Definition of the Stanford Accident Cost Accounting System

The Stanford Accident Cost Accounting System can be defined as a management system which increases supervisory accountability for safety performance by immediately measuring and highlighting accident costs.

The system was developed to provide contractors with a method for tracking accident costs along with their other costs on each project. Since costs are a guiding concern in running jobs, project managers, superintendents, and foremen respond to those items which have been translated into costs and are on the job cost sheets. The Accident Cost Accounting System is designed to make accident costs visible to all levels of management.

Difficulties with Using Claim Costs

The principal reason why most contractors have not already included at least insurance claims costs in with their other costs is that accident costs have a very substantial time lag. The total costs of an injured back today, for example, may not be known for many years. *But these costs still have to be paid by the contractor.*

Robinson developed a system which can estimate the total costs of accidents at the time of their occurrence, making it possible for these costs to get the attention they deserve on the job site.

Requirements of a Job Accident Cost System

So that it would be usable for construction, Robinson designed an accident cost system to meet the following criteria:

1. Provide timely feedback
2. Accurately reflect accident costs, including hidden costs
3. Be compatible with the present project cost systems
4. Be inexpensive to implement and operate
5. Be simple to understand, implement, and use
6. Be flexible and adaptable for different sizes and types of projects
7. Be comprehensive, able to handle different kinds of accidents

The following sections will (1) describe the Stanford system, (2) evaluate the system to see how well it meets the criteria, and (3) give examples of how companies are using it and what results they have had with it.

Description of the Accident Cost Accounting System

Robinson's goal was to develop a method "which would provide the construction manager with a schedule of costs which are a function of some easily and quickly determined variables arising from the accident" (Robinson, 1979, p. 26).

The schedule he developed uses three variables: (1) part of body injured, (2) nature of the injury, and (3) whether or not the injury resulted in one or more lost workdays.

In order to provide accurate predictive cost data, Robinson first obtained workers' compensation insurance claims costs for several thousand construction accidents that occurred on a wide variety of construction jobs in different parts of the country over a 3-year period.

He next classified the claims costs into categories using part of body injured (head, neck, arm, etc.), type of injury (fracture, cut, sprain, etc.), and whether the injury was no lost time or lost time. Data for the various categories were then computer processed, resulting initially in average costs and standard deviations for each of about 500 categories.

The next step was to have an expert in the costs of workers' compensation insurance make estimates of each cost, filling in a blank matrix, as an independent check on the computer data. The computer averages were then compared with the data obtained from this very knowledge-able insurance specialist. The two independent sets of data were generally in close agreement.

The expert and computer data were then combined to provide the best estimates from the two sources, taking into account category sample size and standard deviations. Categories sharing similar costs were next combined, reducing the matrix to seven injury types and thirteen body parts.

The workers' compensation costs for the various types of injuries to the various parts of the body were then adjusted upward to take into account hidden costs. These hidden costs are often expressed as a ratio of the direct claims costs. Since the documented research on hidden costs was not extensive in 1979 when Robinson was conducting his work, he chose a very conservative ratio of 2. Robinson's dollar costs for accidents then were *3 times* the average workers' compensation claims paid for that type of injury to that part of the body. This dollar cost schedule is shown in Table 3.1.

Using the Accident Cost Accounting System

The use of the accident cost schedule is simple enough to be almost self-explanatory. When there is an accident on a job, the part of the body injured and the type of injury will usually be known very soon. If the worker is back on the job by the next day, the accident is no lost time; otherwise it is considered a lost-time accident. It will therefore usually be possible to classify the accident and read off the predicted cost in dollars by the day following the accident.

The following example illustrates how to use the dollar cost schedule:

> Suppose a scaffold plank falls and fractures a carpenter's hand seriously enough to require staying away from work the next day. The predicted cost impact of this injury on the company then can be obtained by reading down the cost schedule (Table 3.1) to "Wrist(s) and hand" and then reading across to "Fracture." Since the carpenter did not return to work the next day, it is a lost-time accident and therefore the second figure is the correct one: $9000.

Robinson developed two rules for interpreting the schedule: (1) for multiple person accidents treat them like a series of single person accidents, adding the costs together and (2) for multiple injuries in one accident, choose the highest cost.

Robinson also recommended that the resulting accident costs found

TABLE 3.1 Accident Cost Schedule (in 1979 Dollars)

Injury type

Body part	Amputation	Strain, sprain, crush, mash, smash Non-lost time	Lost time	Fracture Non-lost time	Lost time	Cut, puncture, laceration Non-lost time	Lost time	Burn Non-lost time	Lost time	Bruise, abrasion Non-lost time	Lost time	Other Non-lost time	Lost time
Head, face	NA	NA	NA	700	8,000	250	3,000	325	7,500	250	1,000	350	6,000
Eye(s)	(1) 45,000 (2) 245,000	NA	NA	NA		250	3,000	200	5,000	300	1,000	300	5,000
Neck and shoulder	NA	350	7,000	1,500	8,000	250	3,000	325	5,000	250	2,000	300	7,000
Arm(s) and elbow(s)	(1) 190,000 (2) 250,000	350	4,000	1,000	6,000	250	3,000	250	5,000	300	3,000	250	6,000
Wrist(s) and hand	(1) 52,000 (2) 250,000	275	2,500	700	9,000	250	3,000	325	5,000	250	4,000	350	8,000
Thumb(s) and finger(s)	8,000 ea. up to 37,000	275	2,500	350	5,000	250	3,000	200	5,000	200	3,000	200	5,000
Back	NA	2,000	10,000	NA	100,000	250	3,000	325	7,500	320	5,000	350	10,000
Chest and lower trunk	NA	450	4,000	NA		250	8,000	325	5,000	250	3,000	250	9,000
Ribs	NA	350	1,000	450	4,000	NA		325	5,000	350	3,000	300	9,000
Hip	NA	NA	3,500	450	12,000	200	3,000	325	5,000	350	5,000	450	4,000
Leg(s) and knees	(1) 89,000 (2) 280,000	375	4,000	500	15,000	250	3,000	325	5,000	250	3,000	300	8,000
Foot (feet) and ankle(s)	(1) 44,000 (2) 90,000	300	2,500	450	9,000	200	2,500	300	3,000	280	1,000	350	2,000
Toe(s)	7,000 ea. up to 40,000	300	1,500	200	2,500	250	3,000	325	2,000	200	1,000	220	2,000
Hernia rupture												200	8,000
Heart attack													30,000
Hearing loss													10,000
Death													90,000

SOURCE: Robinson (1979), p. 34.

from the schedule "appear on the project cost report where they will be highly visible." He suggested that these costs be clearly identified as "accident costs" on a separate line or column of the cost report.

He further suggested that large companies develop their own cost schedules using their own claims data.

Evaluation of the Accident Cost Accounting System

Five years after the publication of Robinson's *Accident Cost Accounting as a Means of Improving Construction Safety*, enough contractors had begun using the Stanford Accident Cost Accounting System to make an evaluation of the system feasible.

This evaluation involved finding out how each company was using the system and what effects they had achieved through it as well as whether or not they had tested the validity of the Stanford Cost Accounting figures against their own claims experience.

The results of this evaluation are described in a technical report by Levitt, Samelson, and Murphy: *Assessment of Contractor Use of the Stanford Accident Cost Accounting System* (1987) and will be summarized here. The report used 13 construction companies that had an average experience with the Stanford Accident Cost Accounting System of over 2 years. The companies ranged in size from one employing 100 workers to one employing 30,000, from one with 1 current project to one having 111 projects. The size of workforce on any project also ranged widely: from 2 to 1500. The yearly dollar volume of the companies varied from $15 million to $2.9 billion. The type of construction work was also very varied: general engineering, underground, building, light industrial and commercial building, highway, and heavy. In addition an offshore oil drilling company and a utility company were included.

This summary will cover the following areas: (1) comparisons between costs estimated from the Accident Cost Accounting Schedule and actual accident costs from companies, (2) how companies use the system to create accountability, and (3) results companies have gained from use of the system.

Testing predicted costs against actual costs

Ten out of the thirteen companies made comparisons of their costs as predicted by the Stanford Accident Cost Schedule with their actual costs for the same accidents. All of them used the cost schedule in 1979 dollars (Table 3.1). The usual method of comparison was to take a past year's experience of accidents. Using only the description of the accident, the costs were first predicted using the Stanford schedule and then compared with the actual claims costs as reported by the insurance carrier.

The general conclusion from these comparisons was that the Stanford Accident Cost Schedule in 1979 dollars was a good predictor of claims costs. In other words, the Stanford 1979 dollar cost schedule, which had been developed with a factor for hidden costs no longer predicted any additional costs beyond the insurance claims costs.

After a testing period all but two of the companies studied decided to use the Stanford Accident Cost Accounting Schedule in 1979 dollars without any modifications, despite the fact that the testing showed that it did not cover any additional factor for hidden costs.

One company, however, raised all of the dollar figures in the schedule by 50 percent to provide a small additional factor for hidden costs. Another company updates the schedule on a yearly basis in proportion to the general increase in costs of insurance for the industry.

The primary reason companies gave for continuing with the original dollar schedule was its simplicity. Furthermore, the fact that the schedule predicted only insurance costs without any addition for the many hidden costs did not seem to bother the companies. The general feeling among users of the system was that the whole area of hidden costs was more difficult to justify and explain both to upper management and to supervision. They preferred to keep the costs to those which were most visible: the cost of workers' compensation claims.

Only one company in the group studied followed through on Robinson's suggestion that they compile their own cost schedule using the Stanford one as a model. This company, a large utility company with resources beyond those available to most construction companies, used over 13,700 employee injuries as a computer database for determining the average claims cost for each injury classified in the matrix. They also undertook a separate study of indirect costs for a sample of their accidents. From this study, they concluded that their indirect costs were approximately 6 times their direct claims cost for an average accident.

Using their own data for claims cost and their own multiplier of 6, they then developed their own revised accident cost schedule.

Summary of changes made by companies in the cost schedule

As we have just seen, most companies are using the dollar cost schedule (Table 3.1) without any modifications after having compared the costs predicted by the schedule with their insurance claims costs for the same period. One company revises the schedule upward yearly to take into account general increases in insurance assessments, another has revised the schedule to provide a small factor for noninsured hidden costs, and one has used its own data to make a company version of the accident cost schedule.

In addition, some companies have made minor changes in the schedule to reflect regional changes in death benefits and to compensate for conditions not covered in the original matrix.

Uses of the Accident Cost Accounting System

The Accident Cost Accounting System was developed to provide a means for increasing supervisory accountability for accidents. How did the companies use the system once they had introduced it? There are two parts to this question: (1) What kind of reports are they generating with the accident cost schedule? and (2) Who receives the reports and what do they use them for?

The larger companies with sophisticated computer capability are using the Accident Cost Accounting Schedule to generate a large number of different measures, while smaller companies without computers concentrate on a few basic measures.

The most widely used measure is accident costs per employee hour worked. Most of the companies studied obtain accident costs per employee hour worked for each project on at least a monthly basis. Many of them obtain accident costs per employee hour worked for each one of their supervisors, including foremen, on a monthly basis. In larger companies these figures are combined to provide comparisons among all projects, among divisions, and among larger units. The cost figures are usually organized so that it is easy to make comparisons among foremen, superintendents, and project managers on their relative accident costs.

Two companies have developed very detailed and extensive records by which accident costs can be monitored by foremen, project, area, date, accident type, and body part.

Most of these reports are not part of the usual project cost reports as Robinson had hoped they would be in order to keep accident costs very visible on construction sites. Instead, they are usually issued as separate reports. Two companies in the group studied, however, have included the Stanford Accident Cost Accounting System cost data in their estimates of the profit of a project. Both of them replace the predicted costs with claims costs as reported from their insurance companies as soon as they become available. Another of the companies is planning to introduce a method of including the accident costs in job costs.

The question, "To whom are reports sent within the company?", received a variety of answers. In all cases upper management received reports using data from the Accident Cost Accounting Schedule. Usually all projects also received reports. In a number of cases all superintendents received the monthly list of superintendents ranked in order of decreasing accident costs. This was also sent to all members of upper management.

Effects of the Stanford Accident Cost Accounting System

If we look at both the types of reports issued using the system and the people who received the reports, we can gauge the degree to which the system is operating to pinpoint accountability for accidents costs. The results of this study indicate that it is indeed operating as a way to establish accountability. In all companies comparisons among supervisors on accident costs are a built-in part of the use of the system. And since the data are also summarized for larger units such as projects and even divisions, middle managers, as well as upper management, are made highly aware of their standing in relation to others and their absolute level of accident costs. The results of the follow-up study indicate that accountability for accidents is being fostered through the Stanford Accident Cost Accounting System.

The central importance of reports being reviewed by the president of the company was underlined by the experience of one of the companies in the follow-up study.

The son of the president of Slocum Construction Company, whose father had made him a company vice president, was very interested in computer applications to construction and immediately began tracking accident costs after he learned of the Stanford Accident Cost Accounting System. A year later one of the researchers on the study called the vice president to discover how the system was being used and was disappointed to learn that a great deal of interesting information was being generated, but the supervisors were not receiving any of this information. The president told his son that accident costs were covered by insurance and that they were an expected cost of the construction business.

Another year passed before the researcher called again. The vice president stated that his father was now taking the figures seriously and had begun to inquire about accidents every time he visited a job.

Even though the reports were still not being sent to the jobs, accidents began to drop systematically as soon as the president began to expect accountability for accident costs as well as other costs!

Each company was also asked to state any effects which they felt the system had had on the company. Nine out of the thirteen companies volunteered that the system had increased awareness of accident costs in their company. Some of them described it as "more company awareness" or "more awareness of accident costs by all personnel"; others stressed awareness of one group: "upper management awareness" or "supervisory awareness" or "greater injury cost awareness in the field."

Other effects noted were that the system had created an attitude in the company that safety was a line responsibility rather than a top management and staff responsibility, that it had simplified the accounting for and tracking of accidents, and that it helped to identify trends so that management was able to pinpoint problems and develop better solutions.

Most of those answering the evaluation questionnaire were safety directors for their companies. They were usually not willing to answer in terms of whether or not the Stanford system had affected insurance costs or their experience modification rating. Their reason was that they had not only introduced the Stanford system but had also made other changes during the same period and thus could not gauge the independent effect of the Stanford system.

Two respondents introduced the Stanford system without any other changes so they were able to measure its effect on costs. They were a safety consultant and a project manager who was also charged with responsibility for the company's safety program. The safety consultant indicated that the Stanford Accident Cost Accounting System had saved his clients a million dollars. The project manager indicated that by the introduction of the Stanford Accident Cost Accounting System the company's experience modification rating had been lowered from 100 to 40.

Summary of Evaluation of the Accident Cost Accounting System

The follow-up study of companies using the Accident Cost Accounting System showed:

1. Costs estimated from the Stanford schedule are an accurate reflection of insurance claims costs but are too low to reflect hidden costs.

2. Companies are using the system for a variety of comparisons on a weekly, monthly, and quarterly basis.

3. The most frequently used single measure developed from the schedule was *accident costs per employee hour worked* which was calculated for foremen, superintendents, projects, divisions, etc.

4. Putting the Stanford schedule on a computer meant that accident cost records could be kept by supervisor, job, accident type, body

part, etc., yet even companies not using computers were able to use the schedule very effectively.

5. Generally accident cost reports were sent to the president and other top management people and to each project, but some companies also sent them to all supervisors or even to all personnel.

6. Companies using the system felt that it created greater awareness of the cost of accidents.

7. The few evaluators who were able to test the specific impact of the Stanford Accident Cost Accounting System attributed substantial reductions in insurance costs to its adoption.

The evaluation indicated that the companies found the system useful, adaptable to their own organizations, and effective in increasing supervisory awareness and motivation to improve safety performance.

Summary of How Safety Saves Money

The fundamental humanitarian motivation for safety management—i.e., reducing human suffering and loss of life in construction—is buttressed by very substantial financial savings from effective safety management.

Workers' Compensation Insurance

- The biggest single cost saving is by paying less for your company's workers' compensation insurance.

- The savings come from lowering your firm's experience modification rating (EMR).

- Your company's EMR is based on its own accident claims costs.

- Each company's annual EMR is based on its accident claims experience for the 3 years prior to the immediate past year.

- The EMR formula weighs the number of claims (frequency) much more heavily than it does the cost of each claim (severity).

- Calculations show that a contractor on a typical $100 million dollar industrial construction project whose EMR was 140 would pay an additional 8.6 percent of his direct labor payroll for workers' compensation insurance coverage than would one whose EMR was 50.

- A national rating bureau calculates the interstate EMRs for those companies working within the 40 states which do not have individual rating bureaus.

- State rating bureaus develop EMRs for those companies working within each of the remaining 10 states.
- In accident cases for which the total costs of the accident are not immediately known, insurance carriers set aside reserves to cover the future claims costs.
- These reserves are sent to the rating bureau in place of the actual claims costs unless the case is closed.
- Monitoring insurance reserves before the unit statistical report is sent by the carrier to the rating bureau will ensure that the costs used in calculating your company's EMR are based on actual claims costs or reasonable reserves.

Hidden Costs

- Each accident also has many hidden costs. These hidden costs, which are often difficult to measure, average at least *4 times* the direct workers' compensation claims cost of an accident.
- Among the easier-to-measure hidden costs of accidents are:

    Transportation

    Costs incurred because of delays which resulted from the accident

    Costs of overtime necessitated by the accident

    Loss of efficiency of the crew

    Cost to break in and teach a replacement worker

    Extra wage cost resulting from lower efficiency of returned worker; cost of clean-up, repair, or replacement material or equipment; and equipment stand-by costs

    Costs to reschedule work

    Costs of wages for supervision as a result of the accident

    Cost for safety and clerical personnel as a result of the accident

    OSHA and civil fines

    Cost of legal assistance

- Non-lost-time accidents, which are often ignored by construction companies in their measures of safety performance, are not only counted heavily in the EMR formula, but they also have proportionally higher hidden costs.
- A conservative estimate of the financial cost of accidents to the construction industry, developed from 1979–80 figures, shows a $19.5 billion a year figure.

- The high costs of accidents to construction companies are avoidable by effective management methods.
- The minimum net savings to be expected from introducing an effective safety program is 4 percent of direct labor costs.

Accounting for Accident Costs

- The first step in controlling costs is to make accident costs visible on construction projects and to hold managers at all levels accountable for these costs.
- A very effective method for making project management immediately aware of accident costs is the Stanford Accident Cost Accounting System.
- The basic tool of this system is an easy-to-use cost schedule which shows costs of nonlost-time and lost-time accidents by part of body and type of injury.
- The Stanford schedule of costs is based on computerized summaries of insurance claims costs.
- Companies can make a company version of the Accident Cost Schedule using their own claims cost information.
- Construction firms which are using the Stanford Accident Cost Accounting System have found that the figures in the schedule predict their insurance claims costs but do not cover hidden costs.
- Most companies studied are using the dollar cost schedule without modification, although some have added minor changes to compensate for conditions not covered or to reflect regional differences in specific benefits.
- Results from users indicate that the system works well as a means for increasing supervisory accountability for accidents and their costs.
- Both companies with sophisticated computer capability and companies without computers have used the system to develop meaningful measures of accident costs to compare projects and supervisors.
- The most widely used measure is accident costs per employee hour worked (accident cost incidence). The companies studied usually keep monthly records of accident cost incidence for each project and for each supervisor.
- Accident cost reports are usually sent to all projects as well as to upper management. Often monthly lists of rankings of superintendents in order of accident cost incidence are also sent to upper management and all superintendents.

- The follow-up evaluation study shows that the Stanford Accident Cost Accounting System fosters accountability for accidents.

- Users state that the system increases management awareness of accident costs and increases line responsibility for safety.

- The few evaluators who tested the specific impact of the system on company costs attributed substantial reductions in accident costs to its adoption.

The Role of
the Chief Executive

It is almost a truism that safety starts at the top. Our research confirms this beyond any doubt. Companies in which the chief executive has a strong concern for safety and communicates this concern to employees by word and deed have better safety records than companies for which this is not true. Furthermore, in companies in which chief executives learn about the benefits of good safety performance (as set out in Part 1) and demonstrate more concern for safety, performance improves— often dramatically.

We have stated that each level of management in a construction organization has a unique and important role to play in achieving high levels of safety performance. This section deals with the crucial role of the chief executive *in establishing the proper organizational setting of goals, policies, and procedures within which line supervisors, assisted by staff experts, can manage safe construction.*

First we need to define "chief executive." In this chapter and those that follow we will define levels of management by their functions instead of by their titles. This is necessary because the functions of the person called chairman, president, vice president, or general superintendent may be quite different in each firm. Our recommendations are grouped according to each manager's function.

We will define a chief executive as a manager who has overall responsibility for the performance of a company or for an autonomous operating division of a major company or public sector agency. Chief executives are held accountable for the performance of their company or division and have the authority to establish policies and procedures that must be followed by all projects. In a small firm there will be only one chief executive who performs these functions. A larger organization with several operating divisions may have several chief executives.

Large or medium-sized firms will often have other managers who work out of the firm's home office and have multiproject responsibilities. These "project executives" or "construction managers" represent the chief executive when they go out to job sites or communicate with project-level personnel. But the individuals who head up construction organizations are the primary focus of this section because research indicates that their actions and decisions have a profound impact on the organization's safety performance.

Three Ways for Chief Executives to Influence Safety

Chief executives are not usually present on projects to supervise construction work. Unlike foremen or job-site managers, they do not normally issue direct instructions to workers or supervise the execution of those instructions. They must therefore influence the behavior of managers and workers throughout the organization in other ways. Our research found that chief executives in the safest companies exert a strong positive influence on their organizations' safety performance in three basic ways:

- *They communicate the message that safety is of critical importance to the company in their direct contacts with employees at all levels and with outside groups. And they have developed ways to do this, in both oral and written communications, that do not undermine the authority and responsibility of line managers.*
- *They place the primary responsibility for safety on line managers. And they hold line managers accountable for the safety of their subordinates.*
- *They require that accounting, safety, and other staff support groups provide needed expertise and resources to the responsible line managers. And they require staff groups to provide safety performance reports to senior managers.*

In this part of the book we are going to set out some specific action steps that chief executives can take in each of these

*three modes of management to create a favorable
organizational setting for safe construction.*

*These recommended actions are the ones practiced by chief
executives in the safest firms in the industry. Moreover,
during the past 15 years, we have seen several firms achieve
measurable improvements in their safety performance when
their chief executives started following these simple action
steps.*

5

Communicating Safety Goals

Understanding the economic benefits of a good safety record has motivated many construction chief executives to strive for this goal. As more construction buyers discover the economic value to them of hiring contractors with good safety records, we believe that excellent safety performance will become an important goal for most construction firms.

In Chapters 6 and 7, we will describe ways that chief executives can improve the safety of their organizations by using proven techniques for managing line and staff employees through the chain of command. However, this is only part of the story. At the same time as they *manage* their organizations for enhanced safety performance, we will show in this chapter how chief executives must also *lead* their employees toward the same goal.

Leadership and Organizational Culture

Management studies of the safest construction firms have found that employees in these firms feel that they are part of a strong "culture" in which safety is given priority. The culture of an organization consists of:

1. A shared view of a higher purpose or meaning to the daily activities of each ordinary employee (Peters and Waterman, 1982)

2. Written and unwritten codes of behavior and conduct in the organization

3. Stories or "legends" about events from the firm's history

An important function of a chief executive is to be a standard bearer of the organizational culture for other employees. How safety concerns fit into this culture is determined by what the chief executive communicates both internally and externally. We will refer to this role of communicating to others what the organization stands for, by both word and deed, as "organizational leadership."

In our industrialized society many people struggle to find meaningful and fulfilling occupations. As a result, workers who do find meaning and purpose in their jobs can be expected to work unusually hard and to be loyal to their organizations. This finding is the essence of Peters and Waterman's (1982) best selling book, *In Search of Excellence*. Research by them and others shows that effective organizational leaders succeed in promoting an organizational culture in which all employees feel that they are part of an organization which:

1. Is broader in its scope and purpose than the confines of their own daily job and routines

2. Has a bigger time span than their daily tasks; i.e., the organization to which they belong has a meaningful history, a present, and a future

Studies of large industrial construction projects reinforce this finding. They find that worker motivation and productivity are highest when each worker is made to feel that he is not just another specialist in a pigeonhole but rather that he is part of an organization that is creating a useful end product with a long life (Borcherding, Samelson, et al., 1980).

> A worker on one of Brown Industrial Constructors' best projects described his job as, "I am building a power plant to light up the Southwest," whereas one of his peers, on another of Brown's projects which was way over budget and 2 years late, described his job as "I am terminating cable connections in area TB-3-1A."

Building a strong organizational culture takes charisma and effort on the part of a chief executive. In addition, both reducing employee turnover and increasing contact between the chief executive and other employees facilitate the development of strong cultures.

In spite of the construction industry's reputation for high rates of turnover, many construction organizations do have strong corporate cultures, replete with legends about heroes and villains, and have strong norms of behavior. Companies like Guy F. Atkinson, Bechtel, C.F. Braun, Dillingham, and Peter Kiewit Sons and agencies like the U.S. Army Corps of Engineers and the Bureau of Reclamation have strong organizational cultures which have persisted long after the departure of the original founders.

The construction organizations cited and many others have developed strong cultures in spite of the cyclical nature of the business. They have found ways to hold onto their key supervisors and workers through the cyclical swings in the economy, sometimes loaning foremen or superintendents to competitors temporarily in order to retain their links to these "human assets."

In these organizations with strong cultures, most managers have also risen through the professional or craft ranks and have come into contact with a wide range of personnel on the way up, absorbing the culture in the process. Furthermore, many of these construction firms were founded by one or two managers, usually with no outside investors, and have remained closely held by their senior employees. This further contributes to a feeling of ownership and belonging. Employees in organizations that have this type of strong culture are often fiercely loyal to it and will try hard to achieve the purposes and objectives of the organization, as these are communicated to them by its leaders.

A company can improve its safety performance—sometimes dramatically—by managing through the line and by harnessing staff support for safety. However, to excel in the area of construction safety, it is also necessary for the chief executive in an organization to exercise the leadership skills necessary to build and maintain a strong corporate culture in which safety is given a high position.

Communicating Safety Goals to Employees

A leader who believes in safety gives direct evidence of this by holding all managers accountable for the safety of every one of their subordinates and by being willing to commit real and substantial organizational resources to training, monitoring, and other safety-related activities. However, in addition to these direct actions which we detail in the following two chapters, a leader can give indirect, but equally important, indications of concern that safety should be part of the organization's culture. In the remainder of this section, we will give some examples of how chief executives in the safest companies communicate safety goals to their employees and to outsiders.

Promoting the right people

The kind of people who are promoted into managerial positions is one of the most powerful indicators of organizational priorities for employees. We will describe in Chapter 6 how promotion can and should be a reward for managing safe construction. The attitudes and behavior of newly promoted managers are likely to be emulated by others seeking promotion. This "copycat" effect of promotions on the behavior of others may be even more important than the direct motivational effect. We found that chief executives in the safest companies ensure that newly hired or promoted managers hold a deep and honest concern for safety.

In HOS, a medium-sized heavy construction firm which we studied, hiring the wrong manager had a strong negative impact on a company that had been improving its safety record in many of the other ways cited above. The aging principal of this firm brought in a young, technically competent manager to take over the firm's operations so he could start to reduce his own commitments to the firm. This younger manager felt that the firm had been overemphasizing safety at the expense of costs and schedules, and he said so on many occasions. Even though the firm had already implemented, and continued to follow, many of the safety practices that we recommend in this book, its safety performance took a steep nosedive. Two years later, the firm's experience modification rating caught up with it, and it began to experience severe difficulties in competitive bidding, especially for underground work for which workers' compensation insurance premiums average around 30 percent of labor costs.

Talking about safety on job visits

Virtually all of the safest firms' chief executives told us that they made a point of talking about safety on job visits. When chief executives go out onto a project, they are presented with an opportunity to show that they know about the safety record of the project and that they want it to be good. Questions about a past accident and what has been done to remedy the hazard, praise for a good safety record, or a comment about the safety environment of the project all serve to deliver the message that top management cares about safety.

Astute chief executives can do this in a way that serves to communicate the organization's goals without undercutting the authority of job-site management. Telling a foreman that safety is important in the presence of a project superintendent can serve to bolster, rather than undermine, the superintendent's authority. This process by which chief executives communicate the organization's goals to employees through direct comments made on job-site visits is a key part of what Peters and Waterman (1982) refer to as "managing by walking around."

The chief executive of Pike, a large, very safe marine construction company told us, "If I always asked about costs and schedules when I visited projects and sent the jobs letters or brochures telling them to be safe in between visits, they would correctly infer that the safety letters or brochures were just window dressing and that what I really cared about were the things that I discussed with them in person. So the first thing that I discuss when I meet with a superintendent or foreman on a job is his safety record. That way he knows its my top priority." .

Taking time to attend safety functions

Another way that chief executives can communicate the importance that they attach to safety is by "putting their time where their mouth is"—i.e., by taking the time to attend safety meetings or functions with other employees.

The president of RRS, a medium-sized building contractor, always shows up at the firm's monthly safety breakfast. He takes the safety quiz that is administered prior to breakfast and reads out the ranking of projects in terms of accident frequency. Obviously this sends a very strong signal to superintendents and foremen who attend these meetings, and the results bear it out. This firm has a remarkably good safety record. Its experience modification rating is around 50 percent.

Using written communications to promote safety

Written communications which originate from the chief executive of an organization are also effective ways to communicate their concerns and priorities. In many organizations, a statement from the current chief executive of what the organization is about and what its guiding principles are is issued to all new employees at the time that they are hired. A strongly worded section on safety is included in such an introductory letter by many of the safest firms in the industry. A letter like this followed by a thorough orientation session that includes a slide or videotape message from the president and discusses recommended safety practices sets a tone for all new employees which says: "Safety really counts here!"

Personal letters do not have to stop after a new employee is hired. The president of RRS noticed that his company's outstanding safety performance had slipped just a little during the past year. He sent out a letter with a reply card to each foreman in the firm, asking them to join him in signing a pledge to work toward restoring the company's safety record. This pledge letter got virtually a 100 percent response from the foremen. A number of the foremen turned it in to the president at the company's next safety breakfast.

We have illustrated ways in which chief executives in some of the safest firms in the industry communicate their concern for safety directly to employees. The messages and the media used to communicate the concern for safety vary, but one clear theme emerges among all of these examples: chief executives in the safest firms use both oral and written personal contacts with their employees to communicate that they place a high priority on safety. And they are able to do this without undercutting the authority of line managers.

Communicating Safety Concerns to the Outside

Chief executives in the safest firms also make it a point to communicate safety concerns to outsiders. Participating in industry safety committees or workshops sends a message to peers in other firms that the firm is concerned about safety. Pointing out clearly to subcontractors that the firm will not tolerate unsafe acts or conditions on its projects sends a powerful message to subcontractors that cutting corners on safety is not the way to get hired by this firm. Involving state safety consultants in prejob consultations sends a message to the regulatory agencies that the firm wants to work safely. And discussing safety in contract negotiations with labor unions lets the unions know that the firm cares about safety.

In all of these subtle and not-so-subtle ways, the chief executive defines the culture of the organization. If safety is not a high priority in the corporate culture communicated by the chief executive, job-site superintendents and foremen trying to promote safety start out with one strike against them. On the other hand, when chief executives have placed safety in a high position on the corporate agenda, managers at all levels have a headstart in promoting safe construction through the actions that they can take at their levels.

6

Achieving Safety through Line Managers

In addition to communicating to their employees that they place a high priority on safety, chief executives must educate and motivate line supervisors at all levels to manage safely. In this section we will review techniques used by chief executives in the safest firms to:

1. Establish safety accountability in their organizations
2. Train managers in safe supervisory techniques and workers in safe work practices
3. Require detailed preplanning of work

Establishing Accountability for Safety

We have stated that chief executives, by definition, do not directly supervise work. Rather they set the goals, standards, and performance objectives by which other managers are to be judged, and they then evaluate the degree to which the managers have attained the organizational objectives established for them. It follows that chief executives have an important responsibility to ensure that achievable safety objectives are established and monitored at all levels of the organization. We will refer to this as "establishing accountability for safety" throughout the organization.

A strong safety accountability system exists when:

1. Each manager has a safety goal to meet that he or she believes is achievable.
2. Feedback on progress toward achieving that safety goal is provided on a regular basis both to the manager and to his or her supervisor.

3. There are meaningful rewards for the manager that are associated with meeting the safety goal.

We found that all of these elements of a strong accountability system were present to some degree in the safest firms. Setting up an accountability system for safety in an organization is surprisingly easy to do if its chief executive is committed to the idea. Guidelines follow.

Choosing a measure of safety performance

In order to set, monitor, and respond to objectives in the area of safety, the chief executive must decide how safety performance will be measured. Depending upon the organization's size, the availability of professional safety staff (discussed in Part 5), and the availibility of data about comparable firms, a suitable measure should be chosen and standardized across time and across divisions or departments of the organization.

In Chapter 3, we discuss the strengths and weaknesses of various measures of safety performance. We conclude that *accident costs per workhour supervised* is our preferred safety performance measure. Because of the delay in obtaining actual accident costs, we suggest that organizations use the Stanford Accident Cost Accounting System presented in Chapter 3, or develop a similar set of cost estimates from their own past accident cost data.

In Chapter 21, we provide a detailed discussion of the strengths and weaknesses of various safety performance measures. Whichever safety measure is selected, it is important that it is announced and justified to managers at all levels as being a realistic and significant performance indicator against which they will be evaluated.

Setting safety objectives for senior line managers

Having chosen a safety measure for the organization, a chief executive should then meet with all subordinate line managers and set goals for each manager's safety performance. It should be made clear that line managers are going to be held responsible for the safety of all work carried out in their areas of operations and that they are expected to evaluate their subordinates (superintendent, foreman, etc.) in a similar fashion.

Chief executives should know and expain how safety performance affects the profitability and even the viability of the organization. Then they should translate this into a specific objective that each manager will be expected to meet, with rewards for success and sanctions for failure.

Sam Murray, a project manager, described his firm's approach to us this way: "Our company is determined to bring its experience modification rate down. We have found that safety is a profit maker. We have had jobs which came in ahead of schedule and under budget and yet they lost lots of money for us when the costs of accidents were included. So the company started bonuses for project managers, field superintendents, and project safety people based on the project safety records. To bring down insurance costs the company has set a targeted cost per man-hour for this year which is adjusted to the insurance costs for the state in which the project is located. Next year they will lower the targeted costs. If a project is completed with accident costs lower than the target, the project manager, field superintendent, and safety manager each receive a bonus. There is a lot of competition for these bonuses. Twice a year we all come in and our safety records are read out, and checks are handed to those whose project accident costs were lower than the target. It gets your attention."

Even before the job started, Sam aimed to win that bonus and began the planning that made it happen. Throughout the 18 months of the project he kept track of his progress. He even had the insurance company send him a printout of the project's accident costs every 2 weeks during the course of the project.

Chief executives of the safest companies in our research sample were direct in setting safety objectives for their subordinates. If a subordinate refused to accept safety as a legitimate and controllable performance objective, they would relieve that subordinate of management responsibility.

The group vice president of Branner, a major heavy construction firm with an enviable safety record, put it this way: "If a project manager won't recognize the importance of safety performance and his responsibility to manage for it, then he is going to cost us a lot of money in the long run. We don't want this type of manager in charge of our well-trained craftsmen and expensive equipment. It's too big a risk for us to accept!"

In the safest firms which we studied, project managers and superintendents became fiercely proud of their projects' safety performance. They made all craft superintendents, general foremen, and foremen aware that they would be recognized for good safety performance and would be required to explain the sequence of events that allowed any accident to occur.

The result of the goal-setting process should be an ambitious but achievable objective for safety performance that each manager is committed to achieving. If an unrealistically tight standard is imposed, the result—just like for cost or schedule objectives that are impossibly tight—may be to make the manager shrug and say, "Why even try?" But if line managers are convinced that the organization's chief executive truly cares about safety and that they will be able to show their mettle as managers by meeting the challenge to improve performance in this area, the result will be a dramatic improvement in the organization's safety performance. We have seen it happen time after time!

Reporting on safety performance

As the second part of setting up safety accountability in an organization, chief executives need to put in place a reporting system which provides feedback to themselves and to each manager on safety performance. In this way, each manager is provided with a summary of the safety performance of his reporting unit and with a breakdown of the units reporting to him or her.

> Tower, a large building contractor with an extremely good accident record, has its accounting department print an "accident cost per workhour" summary for each project at the end of every month. This is distributed to all project managers and superintendents. This engenders competition among projects to see which will be the safest every month. At the same time, each project manager and superintendent receives a breakdown for his project which reports "accident costs per workhour supervised" for all general foremen and foremen. Finally, a breakdown of his foremen's results is prepared for each general foreman.

Most of the data required to feed such a system is already collected by many construction firms. Accident reports used by many insurance companies and construction firms list the name of the injured worker and the date and nature of the accident; workhour data for each crew is captured from time cards for payroll and labor cost analysis.

An accident cost system such as we propose requires two enhancements to the typical contractor's records:

1. Total workhours supervised by each foreman must be tracked. This can easily be done when time-card data is entered.
2. The name of the injured worker's foreman or supervisor must be recorded on each accident report. The nature of the injury (e.g., leg, fracture) and the responsible supervisor can then be logged into the accident cost reporting system to track the estimated accident cost for that supervisor.

Dividing the accident costs allocated to each supervisor in a given period by the workhours supervised during the same period gives the desired measure.

An accident accountability system like this can be developed in a very short time by a firm's accounting or data processing department. If this type of service is not available in-house, a college student could develop such a system in one summer using one of the popular database programs that are available on microcomputers.

If an organization is small enough so that the chief executive visits all projects frequently and is aware of all accidents, a formal reporting system is not mandatory in order for the CEO to know which supervisors are meeting their safety objectives.

> Massive, a highway bridge builder and one of the safest companies in our study, used no formal reporting of accidents, but project managers knew that they could expect a visit and some detailed questions from the president if an accident occurred on their project. The president of this firm set "zero accident" targets and followed up personally to observe performance.

In spite of the feasibility of an informal system for small organizations, we recommend that chief executives of even the smallest firms set up formal systems to measure and report on safety performance. Formal systems ensure that, even when the action gets hectic, managers will not forget about safety and the costs of accidents, because the reports serve as a constant reminder. With the advent of powerful and inexpensive microcomputers and easy-to-use database languages, the incremental cost of setting up and maintaining formal reporting systems of this type is minimal.

Rewarding the safer managers

Once the safety performance measurement and reporting system is up and running, chief executives must review the reports each period—just as they review cost and schedule status reports—and react to what is in the reports. In this manner, they show that they really care about safety performance.

> Ticonderoga, a very safe heavy-highway contractor, has completely integrated accident cost reporting into its monthly cost reports.
> "We feel that including accident costs in each project's monthly cost reports gives us a truer picture of the profitability of each project to our company," says its president. "Accident costs are paid with the same green dollars as wages or equipment costs; it just takes a while for the accident costs to show up! Once we started to do this, we discovered that some of our 'star' superintendents were actually losing money for the firm."

Whether accident costs are totally integrated into an organization's management reporting system or kept in a separate set of reports, we recommend that chief executives show *personal appreciation* for good or improved safety performance by their senior line managers. This appreciation can be expressed in a few carefully chosen words to the manager on the next site visit, by a personal phone call, or by a warm, personal letter. ·

Beyond giving safer managers a verbal pat on the back for achieving good safety performance, we recommend that such material rewards as bonuses or promotions be made contingent upon excellent safety performance. In our study we found that companies whose chief executives knew which subordinates had the safer records and used this information in bonus and promotion decisions had one-fourth as many accidents as companies in which this was not true! (See Figure 6.1.) Clearly, knowing which managers are safe and using this knowledge to reward them pays big dividends in improved safety performance.

A note on the use of incentive plans for safety

Many firms use incentive systems for their foremen and even for individual journeymen which permit them to earn blue chip stamps, silver dollars, or some other prize by working a week or longer without a lost-time injury. Our research found that, by themselves and lacking other actions by higher management, such incentive programs had little or no impact on safety. Yet many firms swore by such programs and maintained that they were valuable ways to keep people aware and concerned about safety. This puzzled us, so we dug deeper.

We concluded that incentive systems like these, on their own, are ineffective for a subtle but important reason: *accidents to an individual worker are rare events.* A typical construction worker would expect to have one OSHA reportable injury about every 7 to 10 years. Thus a worker who was 10 times as unsafe as the average worker would experience about one OSHA reportable injury per year. An incentive system which rewarded the worker for every week worked without a reportable injury would still reward this very unsafe worker 51 weeks out of every 52!

On the other hand, if one attempts to use a more frequent type of accident—say a first-aid injury to anyone in the worker's crew—as the basis for safety incentives, workers could be induced by their crew members not to report a minor injury in order to preserve the incentive for the group. This is clearly not a desirable result.

Hence we see that incentive systems based on worker safety performance involve a "Catch 22." Serious and clearly identified accidents

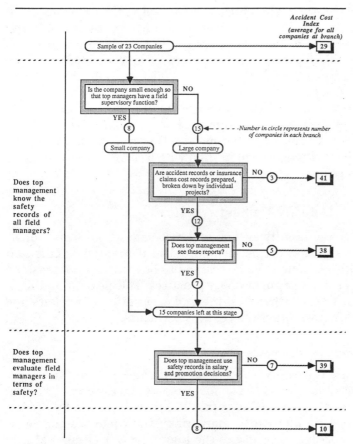

Figure 6.1 Effect of knowledge and evaluation on accident costs.
(SOURCE: *Adapted from R. E. Levitt and H. W. Parker, "Reducing Construction Accidents—Top Management's Role,"* Journal of the Construction Division, ASCE, vol. 102 no. C03, *September 1976, pp. 465–478.*)

are too rare for a worker or a small crew to use them to discriminate between safe and unsafe workers or crews. And less serious accidents can be covered up and not reported. This helps to explain why, when other factors are held constant, crew or journeymen safety incentive systems have little measurable effect on an organization's safety performance.

Yet, if used in combination with a thorough accountability system which monitors safety performance at the project level and provides feedback to managers at all levels about where accidents are occurring, safety incentive systems for foremen and journeymen serve as one more visible sign of management's concern for safety.

We recommend that companies that wish to use such systems base them upon OSHA reportable injuries and award at the superintendent level (or at the general foremen or craft superintendent level on larger projects for which 50 or more workers would be subordinate to such managers). OSHA reportable injuries are clearly defined, and the number of workers covered at this level is sufficient that accidents will not be rare events.

For specialty trades in which crews are small and work on separate sites and for which risks are higher than average (e.g., roofers), crew-based incentives may be appropriate. However, as stated above, they will only be effective in combination with a coordinated, company-wide safety program.

The Importance of Safety Training

Setting up an accountability system will motivate workers and supervisors to achieve good safety performance. But motivation is only half the story; employees must also be trained to be aware of hazards and to know safe working and supervisory practices. The clearest finding of our research on safety is that training and orientation of workers and managers in safe work practices reduces accidents.

New workers are most vulnerable

New workers are especially vulnerable to accidents. Statistics show that *workers who have been on the job 1 month or less account for 25 percent of all construction accidents* (see Figure 6.2). In the first place, construction work is inherently more risky than manufacturing or clerical work. Moreover, because of the high turnover of labor associated with many construction projects, there are always many new workers on a given project. Because of this double jeopardy in construction, it is possible to obtain a dramatic reduction in accidents by simply reducing the risk of injuries to the newest and most vulnerable sector of the construction workforce.

Training new employees in safe work practices

Chapters 11, 15, 18, and 20 contain guidelines for training new workers to be alert and aware of the dangers in the particular construction workplace in which they are being employed and for training foremen in ways to integrate new workers into the workforce. The role of the chief executive in the training area is to see that excellent training programs and materials are developed or acquired for use on projects—either by the firm's safety department or by outside specialists—and to make sure that project managers institute

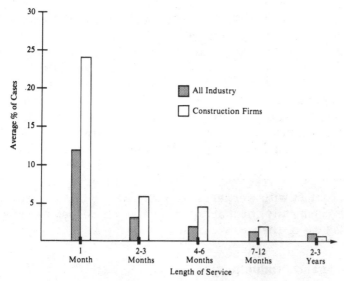

Figure 6.2 Work injuries and illnesses by length of service (state of Maryland, 1976). (SOURCE: *Adapted from N. Root and M. Hoefer, "The First Work Injury Data Available From New BLS Study*, Monthly Labor Review, *January 1979, pp. 76–80.*)

these programs to train each and every new worker employed by the company and each and every newly hired or promoted foreman.

If a chief executive were to pick only one area for action to improve safety, provision of safety training expertise and materials, and enforcement of the regular use of these training materials by new foremen and workers, should be the first priority for action.

> Jackson, one of the safer companies in our study, found that its experience modification rating for workers' compensation insurance dropped by 25 points in 2 years after making only one change in its management practices: the company began requiring thorough safety training for all new hires.

Training supervisors to spot drug or alcohol abuse

Drug and alcohol abuse is currently a subject of great concern to construction managers at all levels. Many firms are considering the use of urinalysis or other tests to screen out workers who might be under the influence of substances which could lead to safety hazards for themselves and their coworkers. This is a controversial topic in which the rights of workers to privacy and freedom of choice in their private behavior are pitted against the rights of the company and its workers to have a safe and productive workplace.

Whatever strategy the firm adopts toward testing of workers, we recommend that supervisors be trained to spot signs of potential substance abuse in their crew members. When a foreman has reason to believe that a worker is drunk or under the influence of marijuana, cocaine, heroin, PCP, or another incapacitating drug, the foreman should be instructed in proper procedures to follow in removing the worker from the job site and in referring the worker to appropriate sources of help.

Chief executives should stress that vigilance in this area by foremen who are in direct contact with workers is the only way to be sure that workers who are chemically incapacitated on the job do not create hazards for themselves or their coworkers.

Planning for Safety and Productivity

Each construction project is unique. This is what makes the industry so stimulating and motivating for all of its participants when compared to the humdrum and routine of manufacturing or clerical industries. At the same time, this means that we cannot depend too much on experience from prior projects to resolve all of the detailed design, erection, and coordination problems on current work. This places a premium on detailed planning of all construction work operations to identify and plan ahead for the unique problems and challenges of each new project.

The large payback in enhanced productivity from the use of detailed planning techniques has been well documented by others (Parker and Oglesby, 1972). However, the benefits of planning in terms of enhanced safety performance are less well known. Our research identified two ways in which planning leads to improved safety performance.

The first way in which planning enhances safety is by identifying in advance any special equipment, tools, or safety devices needed to do a job efficiently and safely. This means that when a new type of work is about to begin, the special items that might be required (e.g., swinging stages, movable hydraulic scaffolds, respirators, etc.) are on hand, checked out, and ready to go. Foremen do not need to improvise with unsuitable equipment to avoid delays; if the correct equipment is on hand the work can be done safely without delay.

The second way in which planning reduces accidents is by eliminating crisis situations which can occur when a crew is suddenly confronted with an unplanned-for situation. Our studies on job-site management show that the stresses caused by crises on a project can lead to accidents. A well-planned operation experiences fewer crises and thus reduces the stress levels for managers and workers alike.

In these two ways, detailed planning of work will lead to improved safety performance. Once again, the role of the chief executive is not so much to carry out a particular action but rather to make sure that the action is carried out by other managers. Chief executives can require that each manager responsible for supervising construction work develop and submit work plans before proceeding with the work.

The intent of such a procedure is not to create a bureaucracy with centralized decision making—we firmly believe that construction work is best conducted with flexible and decentralized decision making. The purpose of enforcing the use of such planning checklists is to create a discipline which forces busy supervisors to take the time to plan.

It is beyond the scope of this book to lay out the format and content of work plans for each level of management on a construction project, but we can provide some guidelines. Each foreman, even on a small job, should be required to produce a weekly plan for the following week and a daily plan for the following day on a simple form which includes the following kinds of planning information:

1. The tasks to be worked on

2. The materials required and their availability and location

3. Any required tools or safety equipment that are not in the crew's gangbox and their location and availability

4. Any drawings or other documentation needed to do the work

5. Any support work from other crews or subcontractors prior to or during the work planned

Construction workers and supervisors are notoriously reluctant to do any paperwork. Thus, a planning process needs to be kept simple and should be facilitated by well-designed forms.

Adherance to this type of planning requirement will pay large dividends in productivity because large amounts of crew waiting time can be eliminated if foremen are required to plan ahead for all of the resources and constraints that affect their planned work (Parker and Oglesby, 1972). At the same time, our research shows that safety performance will be improved in the ways that we have outlined above.

If buyers or other contractors attempt to pressure a contractor to proceed with urgent construction activities without taking the time to plan, chief executives must balk. There is ample evidence that, in this case, more haste is less speed—and people will get hurt trying!

Managing Subcontractor Safety

Many general contractors have taken the position that subcontractor safety is the subcontractor's business. In the past there may have been good legal reasons to avoid involvement in monitoring subcontractors' safety performance. Excessive involvement may have created additional liability. If this was ever good practice in the past, a recent study indicates that it is no longer so.

Under workers' compensation statutes, injured subcontractor employees cannot sue their own employers. As a result, they now frequently attempt to recover settlements in excess of workers' compensation benefits by means of third-party lawsuits against general contractors and construction buyers. A survey by Koch (1984) found that an absence of involvement was no longer a valid defense against such lawsuits for general contractors, construction managers, and project owners. In fact, the opposite now appears to be the case. Failure of a knowledgeable third party to identify and correct a safety hazard is now often the basis for—rather than a defense against—substantial liability awards.

Moreover, accidents to subcontractors' employees cost general contractors real money. Part 1 of this book discusses some of the direct and hidden costs of accidents on construction sites. Many of these costs— particularly those associated with delays—are paid for by the general contractor, even when subcontractors are engaged on a firm fixed-price basis.

Part 6 of this book provides guidelines for construction buyers to use in selecting and monitoring contractors to optimize safety performance. Many of these guidelines can easily be adapted for use by general contractors in their dealings with subcontractors. We encourage chief executives to consider taking this easy step to improved safety performance.

Chief executives, by definition, achieve results through other line and staff managers. This chapter focused on managing through the line organization. We have stressed the importance of developing an accountability system for line managers in which each supervisor is held accountable for the accidents occurring to personnel under his or her supervision.

In addition to motivating managers at all levels to achieve excellent safety performance, the variable nature of construction work and the high turnover rate of workers place a very high premium on training new foremen and workers for safe supervisory and work practices. In addition, foremen should be trained to spot alcohol or drug abusers and to refer them to qualified sources of help. An important function of the chief executive is to see that safety training programs and materials are developed and to get project managers to conduct safety training for all new workers and newly appointed supervisors.

Chief executives should set up procedures to facilitate and enforce planning of work operations by superintendents and foremen. This will pay handsome dividends in both productivity and safety.

Finally, we recommend that chief executives consider selecting subcontractors based upon their safety performance and that they ask their legal counsel to provide project personnel with current guidelines for appropriate degrees of involvement in monitoring subcontractor safety compliance and in correcting observed safety deficiencies.

Chapter

7

Managing Staff Support for Safety

The safest construction companies treat safety as a line responsibility and regard safety performance as one of the measures by which line managers at all levels are evaluated. However, there are important staff roles in these firms, too. Staff personnel in the safest firms:

1. Support line managers in their efforts to achieve good safety performance
2. Assist chief executives in monitoring the safety performance of line managers

This chapter presents approaches used by the safest companies to provide and focus specialized staff support on improving construction safety.

Focusing the Accounting Function on Safety

In most organizations which have a management information system (MIS) function, it grew out of the accounting department's requirements for automated payroll, billing, and payment procedures. As a result, the MIS function often remains under the control of accounting and operates to serve its needs. Reports of a nonfinancial nature are provided as adjuncts or extensions to financial reports, and forecasts or other "soft" data are not permitted to "contaminate" the accounting system. As a result of this regrettable—but widespread—situation, many MISs are relatively useless collections of data for purposes of management control.

Worse yet, many accounting systems not only fail to inform managers, they may actually mislead them! The accounting system, by the creed of the profession, measures those costs which have accrued up through the current period and whose magnitude can be assessed in an objective and verifiable way. In many organizations, the accounting system has no way to measure the organization's performance in terms of certain important management objectives that may have real value or cost over the long term but which cannot be measured by accounting standards on an ongoing basis.

Quality, safety, and customer satisfaction are three performance areas in which ongoing failures can have disastrous long-term impacts. Yet the typical accounting system has no way to measure, record, and project into the future the value of success or failure in these areas.

In this insidious way, emphasis on controlling current period "costs" as recorded by the accounting system can lead to suboptimization in a number of important areas. The lack of customer follow-up is one, underemphasis on control of quality is another, and underinvestment in safety is a third. *In all of these areas, the costs involved in improving performance are captured by the system, but the increased value to the organization of improved performance is not.*

These shortcomings of management information systems may not be too important in smaller organizations in which senior management has many informal ways to measure client satisfaction, product quality, or safety. However, in larger organizations in which the formal control system becomes more important in evaluating the performance of managers, a MIS which is driven by traditional accounting principles will create strong incentives for managers at all levels to underinvest in safety, quality control, and customer satisfaction.

Some of the actions suggested in this book require an investment of up-front financial resources in order to reduce the organization's cost of doing business over the long haul. We recommend that the chief executive take steps to eliminate the natural bias toward underinvestment in safety in two ways:

1. Make it painless for line managers to invest in safety training, safety equipment, and other safety measures
2. Make the costs of poor safety performance highly visible

The first step can be accomplished by allocating a generous budget to projects for safety. An even better approach, which is followed by some of the safest companies we surveyed, is to permit projects to charge bona fide safety expenditures to a corporate safety account.

On reimbursable cost projects, contractors are naturally reluctant to do this. They would rather have such costs reimbursed in full by the client and will therefore try to get them included in field reimbursable costs. As a result of the Business Roundtable's work in this area, many clients are becoming more sophisticated about the benefits to them of good construction safety performance and are often willing to support such expenses at a generous level in the project's reimbursable overhead costs (Business Roundtable, 1982).

A knowledgeable client will create contractual terms that give the contractor no incentive—not even a misguided short term incentive—to skimp on safety expenditures. Removing safety expenditures from the category of "nonreimbursable contractor home-office overhead and profit" should be mandatory for any enlightened client. Chief executives of construction firms should attempt to persuade their clients to provide full reimbursement for bona fide safety expenses, using the Business Roundtable (1982) report and this book as ammunition, if necessary.

At the same time, executives in both client and contractor organizations should work to make the costs of accidents as visible as they can be. We explained in Chapter 1 that the workers' compensation system takes 2 years to begin to recognize the costs of past accidents in current premiums. Even then, the past costs are spread over 3 years and the effects of individual, severe accidents are dampened out by the rating formula. Moreover insurance costs represent only about 40 percent of the costs of construction accidents (see Chapter 2). As a result, unless special efforts are made to highlight them, the true costs of their accidents are not visible to line managers and to the chief executives to whom they report.

During our first study of top management's effect on safety (Levitt, 1975), we found two firms that were attempting to estimate the costs of accidents and to show these costs as charges against each project. These were two of the safest firms in the industry. We, therefore, decided to develop a system that other firms could use for estimating their own accident costs at the time that accidents occurred. The result was the development of the Stanford Accident Cost Accounting System by Michal Robinson (1978). This tool is described in more detail in Chapter 3.

Using the Stanford system, or actual accident costs obtained from a firm's workers' compensation carrier, it is possible for any organization's accounting or data processing department to track and make visible the costs of its accidents. Construction has always been a very cost-conscious industry. Our experience has shown that when foremen and superintendents start to see what accidents really cost the firm, they develop a heightened concern for preventing them.

We have shown that traditional accounting procedures lead to a bias against safety. Organizations that recognize this can use their accounting or data processing departments to focus the organization's attention on safety by requiring that they track current, estimated costs of accidents, rather than "actual accounting period costs."

As we discussed in the previous chapter, such an accident cost accounting system is a prerequisite for developing strong safety accountability among line managers. The accounting or MIS department must support this objective. At the same time, it can help to institute procedures that will make it as easy as possible for line managers to charge bona fide safety costs on both hard money and reimbursable cost projects.

Getting the Most from the Safety Staff

If an organization is large enough to support a safety department, skilled professionals who are specialists in construction safety and health can give the organization a significant advantage in achieving excellent safety performance (Levitt, 1975). When firms are too small to justify a full-time safety professional, part-time consultants can prove valuable.

We have stressed that safety should be regarded as a line responsibility, but there are many ways in which safety professionals can assist line managers to work safely. Part 5 of this book sets out some detailed guidelines for getting the maximum benefit from a construction organization's safety staff. In this chapter, we discuss how chief executives can establish their proper role in the organization. This will determine the way in which they interact with line managers and their ultimate effectiveness.

A perennial problem for safety professionals in construction is developing influence and "clout" with field construction supervisors. Since safety professionals are staff, they have no formal authority to give directives to line managers. Rather, they must rely on the power that comes indirectly from senior management support of their role and on the level of informal authority that they can develop.

We have observed that an important source of power for field safety representatives is their expertise. This so-called "expert authority" is needed by a staff specialist who must go out on to a project that is filled with aggressive line managers trying to get the job done. Even if the chief executive says that a safety representative has the authority to shut down an unsafe operation or an unsafe project—and we recommend that this authority be given—it will rarely be used by safety representatives unless they feel confident in their judgment that there does indeed exist a condition of imminent danger. One bad call could lose the representative and his or her boss, the corporate safety director, a great deal of the respect that both need to get compliance and support from line managers. Only a well-trained and experienced safety representative will have the confidence to demand that safety infractions be corrected or to shut down work where imminent danger exists.

If an organization is going to have a safety department, chief executives need to recruit (internally or externally) and train top-notch individuals to be their professional safety staffers. The old approach of "making an ex-carpenter with a back injury the safety engineer" without giving this person any formal training in construction safety is likely to do little for safety in the organization. In contrast, a knowledgeable, respected, and diplomatic safety representative can be a real asset to a project in many ways other than safety.

One of the authors was employed on a nuclear power plant project on which the safety representative averted a potentially serious jurisdictional dispute. The ironworkers were about to walk off the project in protest of the fact that a carpenter had welded himself a metal handrail for a suspended scaffold on which he was about to work. The 60-year-old safety engineer confronted the 6-foot, 250-pound ironworker steward and asked in a jocular voice, "Hey, Joe, you wouldn't let this dumb carpenter build you a wood scaffold if you had to work up at 200 feet, would you? Knock it off and go back to work." The workers roared with laughter and the situation was instantly defused.

A safety department of well-trained and energetic people with excellent interpersonal skills should be formed. These safety specialists must be thoroughly trained in all aspects of construction work methods and safety practices, with particular focus on the organization's type of construction work. And they must be given funds to attend workshops and seminars so that they stay abreast of new developments in the law and in technologies for accident prevention, training, and motivation. It must be made clear that safety representatives can have a significant and important role in the firm and that the position is not a dead-end alley. The scope of a successful safety manager's job can be expanded over time to include coordination of all types of insurance (often termed "risk management"), labor relations, or other areas which are connected to safety.

Chief executives should be aware that the caliber of the people appointed as safety representatives in a firm sends a strong signal to everyone in the organization about safety's place in the corporate culture. Appointing capable and well-trained people to these positions sends the signal that safety is high on the corporate agenda.

Professional safety staff of high caliber will build up their own base of informal authority and respect in the organization and will be sought after by line managers for assistance and counsel. The benefits to an organization of an effective safety department can be substantial. Our research found that, in comparable-sized firms, those with corporate safety departments had EMRs which averaged 14 percent lower than their counterparts that did not have safety staff (Levitt, 1975, p. 82).

We believe that safety is first and foremost a line function and that safety should be one of the important measures of each line supervisor's performance by which he or she is judged. The role of staff units in construction firms must, therefore, be to assist the line in managing safely and to aid chief executives in evaluating the safety performance of line managers.

Traditional accounting measures do not capture current accident costs, and they lead to a bias against investing in measures that will improve safety. Consequently, chief executives must require their accounting departments to develop more meaningful, albeit non-traditional, accident cost measures (such as the Stanford Accident Accounting System) and to collect and disseminate safety results in terms of these measures. This is a prerequisite for establishing strong safety accountability of line managers.

Where firms choose to have in-house safety specialists, the degree of authority that these specialists will command is directly related to their expertise and to the backing that they receive from the chief executive. It is, therefore, essential that the safety staff is made up of trained and capable experts in construction safety and that it is provided with moral and financial support by the chief executive to stay well informed. Appointing such people as safety staff will reinforce the importance of safety in the organization's corporate culture. Moreover, their expertise and competence, along with top management support, will give them the personal power that they need to function as effective support to the line organization.

8

Summary of Action Steps for Chief Executives

Chief executives of a construction firm do not directly supervise construction workers on a daily basis. Nevertheless, by the image that they project and by their behavior on and off the projects, they have a greater impact on the firm's safety performance than any other managers. Chief executives affect the firm's safety performance in three ways:

1. They create an organizational culture in which safety is a high priority.
2. They hold line managers directly accountable for the safety of their subordinates.
3. They provide and focus staff support to help line managers meet their safety goals.

Building a Safety Culture

High-performing organizations with strong cultures are created by managers who inspire others to share their goals. The chief executive of a construction firm must *lead* as well as *manage* in the area of safety.

1. Promote the right people—those who show by their actions and their words that they share your goal of outstanding safety performance. This rewards the safest managers and sends a powerful signal to others.
2. Communicate the message that safety is of critical importance in direct contacts with employees at all levels.
   a. Talk about safety on job visits; this sends the message that safety is a high priority.

b. Take the time to attend safety functions.

c. Write personal letters of congratulation to managers who achieve unusually good safety performance.

Getting Safety from Line Managers

Line managers at all levels must be held accountable for the safety of those they supervise. This is the key to running a safe construction firm. In addition, workers must know how to work safely, supervisors must know safe methods of supervision, and work operations must be thoroughly planned in advance.

1. Set up a strong safety accountability system.
   a. Choose a measure of safety performance that makes sense for your type and scale of operations. We recommend measures based upon accident costs per workhour supervised.
   b. Set ambitious but achievable goals in terms of the chosen safety measure for all managers in the organization.
   c. Have reports produced and distributed that track and compare managers in terms of their safety performance.
   d. Reward the safe managers and let the least safe managers know that they must improve in this area.

2. Twenty-five percent of all construction accidents happen to workers who have been on the job for 1 month or less! Insist on safety training for newly hired workers and for newly appointed foremen.
   a. All workers new to a given job site must receive a thorough orientation to the hazards unique to that job site and to the work operations currently going on.
   b. All newly appointed foremen should be trained to manage crews for safe construction and especially to manage new workers safely.
   c. Whether or not companies conduct drug screening programs, foremen should be trained to spot and deal with situations involving drug or alcohol abuse.

3. Require planning checklists or develop some other mechanism to ensure that all work is planned in advance. This reduces the number of crisis situations and means that essential safety equipment will be available when needed.

4. Consider selecting subcontractors based, in part, on their safety records and have your legal counsel provide up-to-date guidelines for intervening in unsafe subcontract work operations. A "hands off" policy is no longer a legal defense in case of an injury to a subcontractor's worker.

Focusing the Staff on Safety

Safety is first and foremost the responsibility of line managers. However, staff specialists have important roles to play in support of the line managers' efforts to manage safely.

1. The accounting or data processing department must help to establish and maintain the safety accountability system and to eliminate accounting biases against investing in safety. The accounting department must be instructed to:
   a. Assist in defining the best measure of safety performance for line managers at all levels.
   b. Develop the input forms, procedures, and systems to produce reports that track safety performance.
   c. Produce and distribute these reports periodically.
   d. Establish charging procedures that make it as easy as possible for line managers to purchase needed safety equipment on projects.
2. Safety specialists can contribute in many ways to improved safety performance. The chief executive must provide them with the training, financial resources, and personal support to bolster their authority.
   a. Safety representatives rely primarily upon their expert authority in dealing with line managers in the field. They must be well trained or they will be in a very weak position with field managers.

The Job-Site Manager

No one can take the place of job-site managers. The CEO and the other senior managers in the home office, no matter how dedicated and committed they are, must have outstanding safety performance at the job level if the company is to have an excellent safety record and keep accident costs to a minimum.

The basic unit of a construction company is the project or job. No company can be better than its projects. That is where the money in construction is made or lost. It follows from this central fact that effective construction management depends directly upon the on-site person who heads up each construction project. This head of the project carries many different titles in different construction companies and on jobs of different sizes. This person may be called a "project manager," "superintendent," "field superintendent," "job superintendent," "foreman," or "general foreman." Whatever the title—and we shall use "job-site manager"—the manager's job management skills will do much to determine the company's accident level and accident costs.

Through the years many people have conjectured about what job-site managers do to create outstanding safety records. In 1976 Jimmie Hinze published The Effect of Middle Management on Safety in Construction, *bringing this question of effective supervisory methods for job-site managers out of the area of guesswork and into the area of statistical proof. Using the same basic research design as Levitt (1975) did in his study of top managers, Hinze statistically compared the supervisory methods of job-site managers with consistently excellent safety records to those with poorer safety records.*

The next six chapters summarize the results of this research, amplified by our subsequent testing of these findings in construction companies.

Job-site managers with excellent safety records have different management values, goals, and methods than do managers with poorer safety records. The following chapters describe the techniques for project management used by these outstanding managers. They detail their priority systems, their planning methods, their approaches to orientation of new workers, their communication systems, and their methods for working with supervisors, craft workers, safety people, subcontractors, and owners.

Both new and experienced job-site managers, regardless of the size of their job or the number of workers on the job site, should find these techniques practical and easy to apply.

Setting Priorities
on the Job

The secret of superior job-site safety management is a simple one: Treat productivity and safety as two related parts of high job performance. A job-site manager with an excellent safety record who has completed a 350,000 workhour job constructing a complex industrial plant with the extremely low total of only $8000 in medical costs put it this way: "You don't have to sacrifice productivity for safety. The safer the crew works, the quicker they work. The more safety you have, the more productivity you have."

The research conducted on job-site managers comes to the same conclusion. *The safer job-site managers are also the better producers. They are better at keeping down job costs and better at keeping jobs on schedule.* (Hinze, 1976.)

These facts contradict two reasons that managers sometimes use to excuse a poor safety record: Accidents are inevitable in a dangerous industry like construction, and our first priority has to be getting the job done. Such managers are misled by myths, myths that can cost the project and the company a great deal of money. Job-site managers whose projects consistently have outstanding safety records prove that accidents are not inevitable in construction and prove that doing an excellent job on both safety and productivity is an achievable goal.

Highlighting Safety

This goal of safe productive work can best be served by the job-site manager stressing safety. That sounds illogical until one stops and considers that all of the weight of tradition and management methods up to this point has been emphasizing productivity and deemphasizing safety. Therefore, the job-site manager has to put extra emphasis on safety to counteract this long-standing tradition and the many built-in supports for productivity.

A senior project manager of a construction company which specializes in building petrochemical and other large, complex plants tells his staff: "If it can't be done safely, it is not going to be done at all on this job. Safety is most important."

Workers on a new job want to know what is expected of them. They want to know what the real priorities are. Everything about the job must reflect the message clearly.

Very successful job-site managers make communicating the priority of safety to the entire workforce their first task on a new project. They know that reaching every single worker on a project is necessary. Construction is a very decentralized industry; craft workers themselves make many decisions on the job. Examples of worker decision areas which affect safety abound. Two of them are the sequencing of work and the work methods. Only if workers know that safety comes first will they make their decisions so that each job is done in the safest manner.

Another characteristic of construction also makes it imperative to commit each site worker to safety: Job sites have very dynamic, changing environments. Each individual, therefore, has to have the importance of safety in mind in order to continue operating safely under constantly changing conditions. Equipment posing hazards—cranes, trucks, earth-moving equipment—is frequently moved around on a job site. Construction workers do not have an environment like manufacturing in which potentially hazardous equipment is permanently stationed and surrounded by engineered guards. For this reason the job-site manager needs to reach all those working on the site (including subcontractors) and all those servicing the site, such as people delivering materials, with the message of safety's importance to project management.

The job-site manager can never forget the responsibility of keeping everyone's attention on safety. A statement about priorities is imbedded in every action which the manager takes at every stage of a project's life. Keeping safety in the forefront of each person's mind is a continuing, never-ending job throughout the project.

As another outstanding job-site manager put it: "To keep a job safe, you can't just tell people they should be safe. You have to prove that safety is on your mind always, and your actions have to demonstrate that you mean it."

A senior construction manager for an owner who has had experience with both safe and unsafe job-site managers stated this same theme in another way. "Outstanding managers show a deep concern for safety. For them safety is not just lip service. It is not just issuing a memo."

Making Safety a High Priority Early

The priorities on a job begin to be set long before any ground is broken or any craft workers are hired. They are reflected first in the bid and budgeting of the project. Safety has to be budgeted. At this early stage an important decision is what type of safety staff support will be available for the project. On-site safety professionals are necessary when projects are large and/or inaccessible. The decision as to whether the on-site safety person should be a safety professional or a craft worker with special training who is designated for this task depends upon the size and complexity of the job.

A job-site manager reports:

> Even in our jobs, which are probably small in comparison to many of the projects in your surveys, we assign a knowledgeable person, usually a carpenter, as job-site safety coordinator. The coordinator's responsibility is to make a safety inspection of the job twice a day (once in the morning and once in the afternoon), report any unsafe conditions found and direct subs to correct any unsafe methods. These safety coordinators wear special colored hardhats to identify their authority; they have the full support of project management. On our larger projects, this is a full-time assignment—8 hours a day. This cost (really a very good investment) is budgeted into the job at the very beginning.

If the decision is not to have an assigned safety person on the job, effective managers obtain agreements before the project actually begins as to the extent to which the project can count on the use of companywide safety personnel.

Even the way safety protective equipment is budgeted and supplied sends a message about priorities. When provision for excellent and appropriate protective equipment is built into the project budget in a way which makes it easy for project personnel to use such equipment, safety is encouraged. [There is evidence from the top management study (Levitt, 1975) that it is better for the company to make such equipment available without charging the project for individual items—in other words to have protective equipment a part of home office overhead.] Supplying all the safety equipment that is needed is a very visible way to demonstrate company and project commitment to safety.

Job priorities about safety are reflected during planning and at every other stage of job operations. On union jobs, they are reflected in the project or other labor agreements and in prejob discussions. One job-site manager described what they convey to the labor unions in a prejob meeting: "Work on our job but work safely or not at all." A prejob agreement with the unions on this principle lays the groundwork for a cooperative approach to job safety.

Safety Rules on the Job

Safety rules and regulations need to form a part of job procedures. Workers coming on the job learn how to do their jobs effectively— safely and efficiently. They are also told that failure to follow recommended job methods is cause for termination. Effective managers require their superintendents and foremen to enforce these rules with firm and consistent action. Throughout the project the work requirements and the consequences of failure to follow them are spelled out in toolbox meetings and on the job.

Analysis of exposures as jobs progress sometimes show the need for new procedures. On a major bridge redecking project, for example, the project manager communicated safe job procedures appropriate to each stage of the job through $8\frac{1}{2}$ - by 11-inch illustrations and descriptions which were distributed with the paychecks. These new job procedures were sent out just prior to the need for their adoption on the project. Commenting on developing working procedures for each part of the total job, the project manager stated: "I don't think you can differentiate between a good working procedure and a safe one." (Obviously to him only a safe working procedure is a good one.) He also talked about priorities:

> They are hearing from the time they are hired on a daily basis: "We are going to do the job safe." They don't have to guess what we mean. Through words and deeds, we send the signal: We do care.

Importance of Personal Commitment

In order for projects to have very good safety records, the job-site managers have to make safety an important goal by their own presence and example. Their willingness to take an active, personal role in ensuring that the job is safe reduces accidents on their projects.

Managers who want safe jobs have to have "safety eyes," be quick to spot safety hazards during their walks around the job, and be sure to report such hazards and problems to their subordinates. They have to demonstrate a commitment to safety so that their staff and workers will take it seriously and build it into their everyday actions.

Managers have to convince their superintendents, general foremen, and foremen to become personally committed to safety on the job. The attitude of superintendents and foremen toward safety directly affects the safety performance of their subordinates. In a study of crew safety (Samelson, 1983), crews who describe their supervisors as personally committed to safety had fewer accidents.

We discussed in the opening chapters how much less visible safety costs are on the usual job than are other types of costs. Even an accountability system such as the Stanford Accident Cost Accounting System cannot stand alone. Safety is a requirement which has to be made very visible, or it will get lost among other demands the job makes on people at all levels. The effective job-site manager is a personal champion of safety.

There are various means for increasing safety visibility. One of them is through housekeeping. One project manager whom we know is an expert at turning around jobs which have gone sour. This manager always starts by improving housekeeping from the very first day on the project. Requiring everyone to store materials neatly, pick up trash, etc., immediately creates a new, safe look to the project. It convinces the workers that the project manager's commitment to job safety is genuine.

Even though effective construction safety management involves much more than a willingness to meet basic OSHA requirements, the enforcement of OSHA requirements is another way to demonstrate safety commitment to workers. When Hinze (1976) asked managers to suppose that an OSHA inspector came on the job and then to decide if there were any logical items that they might be cited on, he found that the managers who answered No to that question had significantly better safety records than those answering Yes. Those saying Yes often followed it with such comments as "they always can," "they could find something to cite on any job." Job-site managers with such attitudes are likely to permit more hazardous conditions on their jobs and also to convey both to their staff and to the workers that safety is not an important goal on the project.

Signals to Subordinates

Job-site managers make known their involvement in safety not only through their housekeeping rules and their enforcement of OSHA requirements but also in their expectations of their subordinates. Safety will not be considered a high priority on the job if unsafe behavior is condoned.

The effective manager works with superintendents on job safety questions and expects them to require safe behavior of the people they supervise. Enforced standards for safe behavior on the project pay off in lowered accident levels.

Job-site managers who attend safety meetings for the craft workers demonstrate to the workers that project safety is worth the time taken from their busy schedules. Their attendance at safety meetings also keeps those conducting the meetings from falling into comfortable ruts. The supervisors realize that they must use their time effectively. A job-site manager whose company has an excellent safety record describes one good way of handling safety meetings: "We hold weekly job-site safety meetings, and all job-site project management attend them."

Job-site managers also signal the importance of safety by their attitudes toward safety representatives and safety professionals. The manager who supports the recommendations and role on the job of safety staff shows job personnel that these staff members speak for project management. Through these actions, the job-site manager reinforces the importance of safety considerations to the effective running of the job. No one will fail to take seriously a safety representative or professional with that type of solid backing.

Signals to Subcontractors

Job-site managers who will be working with subcontractors need to meet with them before they come on the job to make sure that they understand that safety is a central requirement on the project. Although clauses on safe practices and procedures are a usual part of contracts with subcontractors, these statements are often seen primarily as a protection for the general contractor against lawsuits rather than a demand that the subcontractor's operations be carried out safely.

Managers who discuss safety considerations at all meetings with their subcontractors demonstrate to them that safety is a central part of subcontractor's job performance. Inviting subcontractor foremen and craft workers to join projectwide safety meetings also underlies the importance of subcontractors to project safety. Managers should arrange for all subcontractors' activities to be monitored regularly to ensure their continued commitment to safety.

Signals to Buyers

The earliest available signal to buyers concerning a construction company's commitment to safety is its safety record on previous jobs as demonstrated through the company's experience modification ratings and through their OSHA reportable injury rate as compared to competitors. Once the job starts, conscientious buyers monitor the contractor's safety record through the OSHA reportable injuries incidence rate and often also through an accident cost accounting method.

Increasingly buyers are also making formal safety inspections of projects and attending project safety meetings.

There are a number of ways in which job-site managers make buyers aware of project commitment to safety. In meetings with buyers on job progress they include safety questions and problems. They encourage buyer representatives to join job-site safety inspections and safety meetings. They welcome buyer safety audits and suggestions for improving project safety.

Summary

- Make the combined goal of high safety and high productivity your number 1 priority.
- Consider safety in the prebid and budget stage to ensure the availability of safety protective equipment and safety staff personnel on the project.
- In prejob meetings with buyers, subcontractors, and union representatives make clear that the safety-productivity goal will be uppermost on the job.
- Include safety rules and regulations as a part of job rules.
- Inform new hires of job rules and that infractions of job rules are cause for termination.
- Continue to stress job rules on the job and in toolbox meetings.
- Analyze job exposures as work progresses and revise job procedures to keep work safe.
- Constantly show your commitment to keeping the job safe by walking the job with safety eyes: monitoring the job for housekeeping, OSHA requirements, and other unsafe conditions and acts.
- Enforce standards for safe behavior at all times.
- Work directly and cooperatively with the job safety person and let all job personnel know that the safety person represents you out on the job.
- For projects with subs: Keep subcontractors aware of the high priority of safety on the job through job meetings and job walk-arounds; monitor subcontractor safety performance on a continuing basis.
- Demonstrate to the buyer project commitment to high safety performance.

10

Planning for Safe Construction

Construction job-site managers have been accused of spending too much of their time fighting fires rather than taking the time to plan ahead so that there will be fewer fires to fight. To some extent the criticism is justified. Construction attracts an active type of person, a doer rather than a dreamer.

We know from personal experience that planning on construction jobs is difficult. There never seems to be enough time. However, we know too that when people are forced to plan, the time spent is well invested. A colleague of ours, John Borcherding, gives an excellent example:

> The project had been behind schedule and running over budget when a cash shortfall forced the project to close down with only upper staff left, followed by start-up on a shortened work week of 4 days. The forced shutdown gave the project management team plenty of time to plan. When they started up again, the extra day was used for planning. As a result of this more intensive planning, the job came in ahead of schedule and under budget.

Planning is one of the best means for ensuring that safety will be taken into account along with costs, schedules, quality, and other important job goals. If safety is not planned into a job, it will not be there.

The larger and more complex the job, the earlier the planning has to start. Very effective job-site managers on large jobs begin by asking questions of those who developed the cost estimate and the schedule.

This process enables job-site managers to negotiate for changes in the original schedule and costs before their projects are even started. In other words, these managers do not accept the estimate and the schedule and try to live with them; instead they examine them in very great detail to see to what extent they can live with them. And if they find out they need more time and more money, they sell their changes to management and, where appropriate, to the owner before the project starts, backing up their revisions with detailed facts. This means that there are substantial discussions between the project manager and top management and the project manager and the owner before the project begins. Agreements are then reached on costs and schedule.

The advantages of this early negotiation process for safety are enormous. It means that job-site managers can attempt to obtain schedules and costs which they can live with, and therefore they will not feel pressured even before ground has been broken.

Planning is an on-going process on a job. One very effective job-site manager we know separates planning into "big-scale planning," "small rolling-window planning," and "fine-tune planning." Big-scale planning covers such areas as site planning and the development of work procedures for basic tasks including equipment and material usage. It begins before the project starts, but it also continues on a regular basis in order to keep the big picture of the project in mind and up to date. Small rolling-window planning takes a 2-week rolling window of the total job; the coming week is planned and planning is begun on the following week. Fine-tune planning is daily planning for the current week and concerns immediate operations and production.

Job-site managers with excellent safety records give safety a high priority at the big-scale level by working with the safety people before the job starts. One of the main joint tasks is to develop a safety plan for the whole project. This would include, for example, identifying all potential hazards and hazardous operations and deciding on locations for storage of hazardous materials and for on-site medical, nursing, and first aid as well as provisions against fire and for evacuation.

Site planning is part of the big-scale planning process. By developing plans beforehand with the safety people, equipment can be selected and positioned for most effective and safe use. Materials storage and handling can be organized with reference to overall traffic flow and closeness to point of usage. Emergency access routes and procedures can be developed at the same time. The site can then be used more efficiently at each stage of the project.

Working together, the job-site manager and the safety people come up with a specific safety plan for the job. Using the inventory of potential hazards and hazardous operations expected on the job, they develop a set of safety rules and regulations which are then incorporated into the job rules.

This early planning work helps build safety into each job right from the beginning. Combining safety rules with the other rules for the project ensures that all workers joining the project understand that working safely is the only way to do their jobs correctly. Effective job-site managers train their subordinates to impress new workers with the fact that failure to follow the job rules is cause for termination. They also make clear to their subordinates that uniform action is necessary toward infractions of the safety rules. These actions of superintendents and foremen demonstrate to craft workers the seriousness with which the whole project management team views infractions of the safety rules.

Involving Key People

As soon as the job-site management team has been chosen, the manager holds a kick-off meeting of all the key people in the project organization. Among them, in addition to job personnel, may be union and owner representatives.

Working with the union

On union jobs, the job-site manager may want to contact the union representatives to discuss project safety before the job starts. One successful approach companies have developed is to have a clause in the project agreement with the labor unions that requires those who work on the project to use safe job procedures at all times.

A job-site manager from one company with an outstanding safety record uses a prejob meeting with union leaders to make clear the company's commitment to safety. The manager describes how important keeping accident costs low is to the company's competitive position, explaining that a poor safety record could increase the company costs to such an extent that they would price themselves out of the market. This prejob meeting sets the stage for cooperation later if the company is forced to dismiss someone for failure to comply with the safety rules.

Union representatives may also initiate prejob contacts with job-site managers as a part of their program to improve safety for their members on the job. Since reducing construction accidents is a shared goal of both unions and management, cooperation on safety is mutually beneficial.

A representative of a council of county construction unions has developed a prejob conference form to use in discussions with job-site managers and their teams. In addition to details about the project—its type and size; the planned dates for starting, peak employment, and termination; and a list of crafts and subcontractors—the form includes questions about project facilities—parking lot, I.D. tags, check-in gate, drinking water, sanitary facilities—and about the company safety program—toolbox meeting days, first aid facilities, doctor, ambulance, nearest hospital, nearest telephone, whether hard hats are required, special clothing, smoking restrictions, and special safety conditions.

Planning with OSHA

Meeting with OSHA representatives can also be helpful. The early planning process on the large bridge redecking project mentioned previously involved inviting the consultation section of the state OSHA program to meet and discuss the project's potential safety hazards. They were given a walk-through of the job. The job-site manager solicited their comments.

The main idea was to get ideas from them. It also provided an opportunity for us to discuss the OSHA guidelines with them, including those parts which did not quite fit the job. The OSHA consultation people gave their input in writing, and their comments were incorporated in the plans. Some people questioned whether we should open ourselves up to them like that, but I felt the long-term benefits outweighed the risks.

Research Evidence for Benefits of Planning

The results from the separate studies of different supervisory levels are in agreement: Planning has a positive effect on safety. *The Effect of Top Management on Safety in Construction* (Levitt, 1975) reports that those companies which encourage detailed work planning had the safer records. Furthermore those companies in which safety was discussed in weekly job schedule and progress meetings had much lower accident costs than those that did not normally discuss safety in such meetings. The middle management study (Hinze, 1976) found that daily planning meetings with the foremen are more effective for safety than only weekly meetings. The crew study (Samelson, 1983) had a relevant finding: The less safe crews were more likely to consider that job pressures could have been reduced by better planning, suggesting that planning not only decreases the tendency to resort to unsafe shortcuts but also directly decreases job pressures and tensions for the craft workers.

Dangers of Not Following Plans

One of the main causes of serious accidents is the abandonment of plans without due consideration of the original careful thinking that went into them. Under the pressure of time, it is often hard for people to remember all the factors that prompted the original decision. What appears to be a better way to handle the problem may become the reason for a serious accident.

Summary

- Planning will more than pay for itself in job safety, reduced labor and material costs, and improvements in meeting job schedules.
- Planning makes for a safer project by decreasing job hazards and job pressures and tensions.
- Before the job starts, review cost estimates and schedules in detail so that changes in the original schedule and costs can be negotiated with top management and the owner if necessary. This makes the work less stressful and reduces the likelihood of workers taking hazardous shortcuts.
- Keep three types of planning on-going during project operations: large-scale planning, planning for next week, and daily planning for the current week.
- Before the job starts, work with the safety people to develop a safety plan for the whole project.
- Involve key people in prejob discussions. On union jobs involve union representatives; on highly hazardous jobs involve representatives from the consultation service of the OSHA program.
- Discuss safety in weekly job schedule and progress meetings.
- Have daily planning meetings with the project foremen.
- Caution all supervisors and workers about the dangers inherent in last minute changes of plans.

11

Orienting New Workers

> If you just check in a worker, give him a hard hat, and tell him to go out to work, you are telling him that you don't care too much for safety.—Senior construction manager for a large utility company.
>
> We give an orientation to every person whether they are on the job $\frac{1}{2}$ day or a year.—Manager of an 18-month petrochemical project with 300 workers with no lost-time accidents.

The project manager who wants a safe job cannot take for granted that new workers automatically know what to do on the job. Skilled and well trained as most workers are, they cannot know the particular hazards and problems of a construction project that is new to them.

The vulnerability which new workers have for accidents has already been illustrated in Chapter 6, Figure 6.2. As this figure, taken from a Bureau of Labor Statistics study, makes clear, almost 25 percent of all of the construction injuries occur in the *first month* of employment.

Another Bureau of Labor Statistics study shows that while this vulnerability of new hires to accidents is more pronounced in the 16- to 24-year-old age group, it is present in all age groups (BLS, 1982). Clearly orientation is needed to keep new hires from having accidents.

Construction workers even more than those in many other industries are likely to have accidents unless given orientation. The construction environment is filled with potential hazards, no two projects are alike, and each project is constantly changing. That is what makes construction challenging and exciting, but that is also why it is potentially so dangerous. Keeping the project safe depends then on keeping the workers informed and aware. New-worker orientation is a key part of that process.

Methods of New-Worker Orientation

The project manager with an excellent safety record has a well-developed program of supervisor and worker orientation. The particular type of program which a project manager adopts will depend on both the type of job and on the size and complexity of job. Obviously the project manager with a workforce of 1000 cannot have the same amount of personal contact with each new worker as can the project manager with a work force of only 50. There is, however, one basic principle to which effective job-site managers subscribe regardless of the size of their jobs: the way they define which workers need orientation.

Defining who is new

Managers with excellent safety records treat every employee coming on the job as a new employee even if the person has worked for the company or the project manager before.

Furthermore they orient everyone who comes on the site regardless of how long they plan to stay. We are familiar with the sign on construction sites stating "Hard Hats Required." Excellent managers have added another requirement for those coming on the job site: "Orientation Required."

Contact with new workers

Research results show that on smaller jobs, project managers who had direct contact with each new worker had *fewer than half as many accidents* as the project managers who failed to take advantage of this opportunity for direct orientation of new employees (Hinze, 1976).

The project managers who answered Yes to the question "Do you ever become involved with new workers?" described a number of different methods. Some of them interviewed all incoming workers when they were hired. Others made it a point to talk to new workers when they went out and walked the job. Others committed the first names of the new employees to memory in the first few days so that they could greet them personally. All of these methods not only develop a direct relationship between the new worker and the project manager, but they also make evident to the foremen and general foremen the importance of the new worker to the project manager. Job-site managers on large projects can also use some of these methods such as talking to new workers when they walk the job and meeting and shaking the hand of the new workers when they first come on the job. They should also encourage their staff members to contact new workers.

Site orientation

To the job-site manager who has been involved in the project from its beginning, the construction site is familiar and easy to maneuver through. It is not so to new workers. Without management guidance and orientation, it is a bewildering and dangerous place: Today there is a large hole where there was level ground yesterday. Now there is a concrete bucket above you. A moment ago there was clear, blue sky.

New workers need a chance to get their bearings and to learn some of the basic requirements right away. On a small job this purpose can be served by the job-site manager, general foreman, or foreman giving them a short tour.

Some companies use slide-tape or video presentations that are introduced by a member of job-site management. This combination of personal contact with a short presentation, hand tailored to the project and shown to every new employee at the time of hiring, is very effective. The job-site management representative gives the new worker an immediate indication of what is important on the project, a point of view that is then demonstrated to be backed by the company through the slide-tape or video presentation. On big projects a map of the site showing the overall layout and briefly describing the purpose of the project that is given to each employee and site visitor is well worth the investment. The important point is not the use of a particular technique, but the fact that new workers are given site orientation.

Training foremen for orientation

The job-site manager has to delegate the detailed orientation of individual workers to the foremen. It is up to the job-site manager, however, to require foremen to conduct new-worker orientation and to make sure they do it effectively. The research results show that supervisors who reported that their foremen did indeed pay extra attention to the new workers had *fewer than half as many accidents* as the supervisors whose foremen did not pay extra attention to the new workers (Hinze, 1976).

Successful managers make their foremen accountable for new-worker orientation. The manager and the foremen work out together what needs to be included in their orientations for new crew members. The list of specific actions, illustrated in Figure 11.1, provides some suggestions. The items listed on this card summarize the methods used by foremen who have excellent safety records. A number of companies have distributed this card to their foremen as a helpful reminder.

NEW WORKER ACTION STEPS

Everyone new to your crew (no matter how experienced) is a new worker.

1. Ask about last job.
2. Describe the new job.
3. Show worker around site; point out hazards.
4. Introduce worker to the others.
5. Describe your rules.
6. Give worker a test run on tools and equipment.
7. Keep an eye on the new worker during the first few days. Check back to see how the worker is coming along.

From CAL/OSHA Construction Safety Orders: "When a worker is first employed, he/she must be given instructions regarding job hazards, safety precautions and the employer's Code of Safety Practices."   1510 (a)

 166

CREW ACTION STEPS

1. Keep your cool. Anger breeds accidents.
2. When the work's not getting done, find out why; don't just push your workers harder.
3. Keep available to your crew. If possible, watch rather than work.
4. Teach the safe methods.
5. Watch for hazards on your job and correct them immediately.

This material was prepared under the grant number E9FOD432 from the Occupational Safety and Health Administration, U.S. Department of Labor. Points of view or opinions stated in this document do not necessarily reflect the views or policies of the U.S. Department of Labor.

developed by
Stanford University, CE,
Construction Management
Stanford, CA 94305 (415) 497-4447

166

Figure 11.1 Pocket card for foremen.

Elements of New-Worker Orientation

To summarize we will list the key elements of a new-worker orientation program:

1. *Broadening the definition of who is new.* The new employee is anyone new to the project no matter whether he or she has worked for the company, the job-site manager, or the foreman before.

2. *Welcoming the new employee.* Each new employee needs to be welcomed to the job and, even on big jobs, should have an opportunity to shake hands with the job-site manager before receiving more specific orientation from a foreman.

3. *Orienting them to the site.* Some methods for helping new workers become familiar with the job-site are a tour of the site; a personally introduced, project-tailored short slide-tape or video presentation; and a map of the project.

4. *Training the foreman.* The job-site manager needs to make sure that the foremen know (a) that they are required to orient their new workers and (b) how to orient their new workers.

5. *Developing the specifics of job orientation.* The project manager and the foremen should work out together what needs to be included in the orientation the foremen give employees new to their crews.

Extra orientation for apprentices

In the changing environment of construction, with its heavy moving equipment, heights, and other potential hazards, those new workers with little or no previous field experience in construction are even more vulnerable than more experienced new workers.

> A safety professional who, after noting the statistics on higher accident rates for new workers, developed data comparing company accident rates of new apprentices with new workers with more experience reports, "My injury statistics reveal that apprentices are 3 to 6 times more likely to be injured within the first 3 weeks of employment [than new workers with more experience]. We have implemented a program requiring all apprentices to wear red hard hats for their first 30 days and not permitting them to work alone . . . so we can easily recognize them and keep a careful watch over what they do."

Job-site managers with apprentices and other new workers who have little or no previous experience on construction jobs may want to institute these or other measures to help these new workers.

Trade-by-trade and job-by-job orientation

Safety orientation has to be specific to be effective. It is very effective, for example, to tell ironworkers, "On this job, we are going to tie off" and back it up if anyone does not tie off with, "Tie off right now. We do not tolerate not tieing off on this job." Contrast these specifics with, "On this job, we want you to work safely." Such a general statement permits and encourages ironworkers to use their own definition of what it means to work safely.

Another example of specific work procedures as a means for protecting workers on the job comes from the project manager of the bridge job:

> We had work platforms under the bridge where they were busting rivets. Even though the work platforms had toeboards and railings, there was a place at the edge where a worker could fall through. The procedure was that workers beyond a certain point on the platform had to snap off on the safety line even if they were only beyond the point by an inch for a second. Everyone was equipped with a belt and a safety hook which snapped on the safety line. They were required to snap off always. Anyone who did not was given one warning and would be fired next time.

Orientation for Each New Part of the Job

Every time we started a new phase of the work, we got everyone together and demonstrated what was coming up and what the proper procedures were for handling it. And we also put orientation notes in their pay envelopes right before we started the new work—Manager of a high-exposure bridge project.

On complicated work with high potential for accidents, highly effective project managers have found that orientation needs to be a continuing activity that is geared to the work to be done next. Here is another quote from the manager of the bridge project:

> The next phase of the work was close to high-voltage lines which could not be deactivated. The electrical subcontractor taped and flagged the lines red. And then there were prework toolbox meetings where the electrical subcontractor showed the types of cables and how the dangerous ones were color coded and demonstrated to the workers how to work around them. This was done just before they started to work on that section.

Being able to arrange such briefings at the appropriate times in the development of a project depends again on project planning. Certainly step-by-step orientation is the only possibility when the job brings workers into high-risk areas. It is obviously not practical to do more than a general introductory orientation when a worker comes on the job. Not only may the worker be distracted by the new situation, but learning new specific work procedures can only take place after the worker has a background of experience on the job.

Summary

- Organize job and project orientation for all new hires regardless of their years of experience in the work or with the company.
- Welcome each new worker, and then leave the detailed orientation to the worker's foreman.
- Train the foremen to conduct effective new-worker orientation.
- Be sure that foremen talk about job specifics rather than generalities.
- For orientation to the job site on smaller projects be sure a short site tour is included in the new-hire orientation; on larger projects develop a site map that shows the overall layout of the project with a short description of the project.

- Encourage the company to develop a simple slide-tape or video presentation that is introduced by a job-site management representative. This can provide new workers with a good general orientation to the project.

- On those parts of the project that have a high potential for accidents, require orientation prior to each new phase of the work.

12

Maintaining the
Communications Safety Net

Job-site managers with very safe records build fail-safe communication systems. Rather than relying on just one system to obtain and send information, they develop a number of alternative systems. There are three main communication systems: the chain of command system, direct contact, and group meetings.

The Chain of Command System

As expected, managers use the *chain of command system* with which we are all familiar. They communicate with the supervisors under their direction who in turn send the information on to their subordinates. But they do not limit themselves to this system; they also develop and use other systems. They make it clear to all their supervisors that they will also obtain information by other methods. This forestalls the problem of superintendents, general foremen, and foremen feeling that their authority is undermined if the job-site manager uses other communication channels. They use these other systems to obtain information but not to give orders. Alternatives to the chain of command are necessary since the hierarchical approach can be unreliable for upward communication.

Problems of the Chain of Command as the
Sole System

As noted, the chain of command, by itself, is an unreliable system for several reasons. Among them are:

1. Information from the workers has to be relayed through at least two individuals. This introduces distortions. (All of us who have played the game of whispering a statement in at one point in a circle and then hearing the message spoken by the final person know how distorted even simple information becomes with a few repetitions.)

2. The supervisors who are to convey the information may have motivations to protect themselves by not conveying it or by distorting it.

3. The people at any hierarchical level may be unwilling to report to their superiors information that is critical of or shows lapses by themselves or their superiors.

Since information can be distorted and "filtered," the hierarchy may provide very misleading data on which to act.

Direct Contact System

Effective managers also communicate directly with workers. *They walk the job very frequently and feel free to contact and talk directly with any individual on the job.* They can thus obtain evaluations and information from every single person on the project; they also can provide direct information to workers on actions taken to correct problems. During these direct contacts with workers and foremen, they confine themselves to giving and receiving information; they do not issue orders. In this way, they avoid threatening and undermining the chain of command. But, having the opportunity to talk directly with the workers, they can convey to them their project priorities, including the importance of safety to total project performance; they can report on progress; and they can listen to employees' latest safety concerns and explain what they plan to do about them.

This direct contact is the most effective way to demonstrate commitment to safety. As one very successful job-site manager said: "I'm always out there. Three or four times a day. All the workers know who I am. And I attend the weekly toolbox meetings myself. I rotate through the meetings to make sure they are talking safety and not shooting the breeze."

An owner's representative to projects who has observed many job-site managers firsthand comments: "If the project managers don't go out in the field, if they just sit in the office and read safety reports, things just go down and down and get dirtier and dirtier. They have to get out on the job and solicit comments from the workers. They must be seen and heard and listen to the workers. If the workers know that they can talk with you without hurting their jobs, you can find out how safety can be improved on the job and give them a voice in it."

Soliciting comments from workers is an excellent idea; it does require following up with action, however; no one wants to continue to give good suggestions for safety improvements if they are never acted on; inaction is the quickest way to throttle participation.

Nothing can take the place of direct face-to-face contact with craft workers. There are ways, however, to supplement personal interaction.

The owner's representative quoted above also describes another method for direct communication from workers: a hot line on which the worker can call in and raise a question or a problem. This method is especially appropriate on large, complex projects involving a number of units and often different contractors. It allows the craft worker to have direct access to top people who can then follow through on the problem immediately if necessary.

Again, like person-to-person contact, there is the potential for such a method to boomerang; hot-line calls must lead to solutions.

Group Meetings

The effective job-site manager relies on *meetings* with different supervisory groups and with groups of craft workers. These meetings provide a means of contacting members of a group at one time to obtain joint feedback, do planning, and obtain suggestions. Some of these meetings are regularly scheduled, while others may be called for special purposes.

A manager describes one such group for improving communication: "I form a safety committee of all the general foremen. I chair it. Everyone discusses what needs to be done for the upcoming month's work. We get together for dinner. That avoids job interruptions and also makes it informal."

As this example makes clear, meetings are good places for safety planning. Another benefit of group meetings is that they foster communication and cooperation among those attending the meeting. Many times craft groups are not aware of the safety problems which they are creating for other crafts. In intercraft meetings these kinds of problems can be aired and resolved.

Toolbox meetings

One type of meeting which the manager should consider part of the job-site communication system is the toolbox meeting. Highly effective managers make sure that what is discussed at these meetings is directed toward the work the crews are doing; they know what the research evidence shows: the right kind of toolbox meetings can make a difference in the safety performance of the project.

In Hinze's research, superintendents who indicated that the toolbox meetings were primarily used to discuss generalities had poorer safety records than those who mentioned job specifics in describing the topics of their toolbox meeting discussions.

Keeping meeting discussions focused on the particular work that each crew is doing means that the discussions will be relevant and can be helpful. As one safety engineer put it: "Even canned topics can be uncanned if directed to the work at hand and the individuals involved (asking questions and getting feedback)." Job-site managers who require job-specific weekly toolbox meetings are using an inexpensive and effective way to increase safety performance on the job.

Toolbox meetings are a built-in opportunity to provide on-the-job training.

A safety professional from a company with an excellent record comments: "Training can be incorporated into the meetings if it is related to the work, i.e., a demonstration of the correct procedures and equipment needed to erect a safe rolling scaffold on jobs where rolling scaffolds are numerous is a good example."

Successful managers treat toolbox meetings as a continuing method to inform, train, and hear from workers, rather than as a government-mandated ritual. These short weekly meetings are another way to keep communications on safety flowing from and to job management.

Advantages of Multisystem Communication

Managers who rely on three basic avenues to obtain feedback from those working on the project have a much better chance that they will obtain the information which they need. If one method of communication becomes blocked, others are still available to transmit or receive messages on safety.

It is essential that workers have routes beyond the chain of command to communicate their points of view. Job-site managers directly contacting craft workers help to keep the job safe by:

- Receiving information on unsafe conditions which the workers can not correct by themselves

- Gaining direct access to workers for their message that safe job performance is a high priority on the project
- Using feedback from workers to discuss ways to improve project safety with their subordinates and with safety staff members
- Encouraging workers to express worries, dissatisfactions, etc., which otherwise might create tensions on the job and thus lead to accidents

Effective Home Office Relations

Job-site managers have the complex and demanding job of running a construction project, a unique and very dynamic system, and yet they are also a link to the construction company which they represent. Unless the firm is small, they usually have one or more superiors who oversee a number of projects. Does the way in which they handle their relations with the home office have any bearing on the safety performance of the job?

There is evidence to suggest that job-site managers need to be both frequent communicators *and buffers* in order to do a good job on project safety performance.

The managers who talk on the phone with their boss on a daily basis have better safety records than those who talk with them less frequently. There are a number of reasons why frequent telephone contacts with the home office people who are most related to the project could be of assistance to the job's safety performance. In the first place, they are more likely to understand the project if they are kept closely informed of progress, problems, and other job news. Furthermore, the direct and informal reporting process on the phone allows the manager to more easily ask for and obtain needed equipment, supplies, etc. Frequent phone conversations may also keep the home office from asking for formal reports on the status of the project which could add to job pressures.

Being a buffer means that the job-site manager does not pass pressures from the home office on to the personnel on the projects since such pressures can create tensions which can reduce productivity and safety performance.

There is a big difference between goal setting and pressuring. Goals from the home office need to be translated into more specific and immediate goals that are relevant to specific parts of the project. As we have already mentioned in Chapter 9, "Setting Priorities on the Job," goals and their priorities are of major importance to the successful running of the project. By pressuring we mean doggedly repeating goals and deadlines as a means of increasing motivation for them. When project goals are not being met, repeated insistence that they *be met* is what we mean by pressure. Instead, the job-site manager needs to find out why the goals are not being met and how the situation can be changed. Analysis rather than creating pressure is what job-site managers need to do, even though they may be receiving pressure from the home office.

Summary

- Use three communications systems for the job: chain of command, direct contact, and group meetings.
- Train the management team to expect you to use other communication channels than the chain of command to collect information.
- Hold regularly scheduled meetings with supervisory groups.
- Call meetings of different groups, including foremen and craft workers, for special feedback and planning.
- Spend time daily walking the job and talking to craft workers, bringing your commitment to safety directly to the workers and hearing their suggestions.
- Be sure to report what actions were taken as a result of worker suggestions.
- Attend toolbox meetings of different foremen on a rotating basis.
- On a large job, consider installing a hot line on which workers can call in to raise a question or report a problem directly to top people who can then act immediately if necessary. But make sure to get back to workers with an update.
- Train foremen to use weekly toolbox meetings for job-specific safety reminders and safety training.
- Communicate frequently with superiors in the home office to keep them informed of project needs, progress, and problems.
- Do not pass pressures from the home office on to project management and workers.

Chapter
13

People Building

At the heart of the difference between the managers with the safer records and those with the less safe records is their attitude toward their total project staff. On the face of it, most construction workers in the United States and Canada seem to have a series of temporary jobs; they are on the payroll of a company for a particular project and then may or may not be rehired for another since most North American construction companies do not have permanent positions for all of their nonsupervisory personnel. Traditionally, in the construction industry management has not wanted to invest much company time in training and in long-range development of these "temporary" crafts people.

The safe construction managers, however, take quite a different attitude. For them their total workforce, both salaried and hourly, is their most important resource. They value loyalty in their people and work to help them develop. There are a number of research findings which indicate how seriously they consider the task of long-range people building. We have already seen in Chapter 11 that they devote more time to orienting new craft workers and foremen. The research results on job-site managers give many examples of the special "people management" methods used by managers with excellent safety records.

One example from the Hinze study is the finding that those superintendents who were rated by their bosses as "above average" or "excellent" in their working relationships had significantly lower accident rates (Hinze, 1976).

Another way in which the research results point to the higher level of skills in working with people among the safer managers is in the answers to this question Hinze asked: "What is the major problem you have had on this job?" The answers to this question were then categorized into two general classes: physical problems such as rain, material shortages, and late deliveries and people problems, all those dealing with field personnel. Hinze reports:

> The results show that superintendents who reported that people were their major problem had significantly more injuries than those who stated other type of problems were their primary concern (Hinze, 1976, p. 107).

While it is possible that superintendents with more accidents had for that reason more people problems, the likelihood is that the cause-effect relationship is the other way; managers who were less skilled at working with people had more people problems and created conditions which led to more accidents among their people.

Approach to Firing

Firing and the threat of being fired have often been thought of as the job-site manager's most important method for solving employee problems. The results indicate, however, that firing is very carefully avoided among the managers with the safer records. They consider it a last resort.

They give the foremen considerable leeway in hiring, allowing them to choose those who will work directly with them. They do not, however, give the foremen the authority to fire the workers they hire. If the crew member does not work out, the safer managers typically interview both the foreman and the worker and if the two cannot work out their problems, they will often transfer the worker to another crew.

By giving the foremen a considerable say in selecting their crews, the managers recognize the importance of compatability between foremen and workers. By withholding from the foremen the authority to fire, they block the foremen from setting up little empires within the project where their word is law and there is no recourse for the worker. Increasing crew compatibility and decreasing the isolation of workers both improve safety performance.

Those job-site managers who not only keep firing in their own hands (rather than delegating it to their foremen) but also avoid using this authority have better safety records. The managers in Hinze's study were given a hypothetical situation in which they as managers elevate a good worker to the position of foreman on a complicated job only to find that the foreman cannot handle the job. They were then asked: "What would you do?" The job-site managers who answered that they would work with such foremen or transfer them to other work had a much lower average injury frequency on their jobs than those who predicted that they would lay them off or demote them.

Handling Conflicts

Hinze also found that the safer managers listen to both the foreman and the worker when there is a disagreement, another way in which they do not limit themselves to the chain of command communication route. Hinze asked managers what they did about workers who had complaints about their foremen. The managers who said "support the foremen" had much poorer safety records than those who worked to resolve the conflict by listening to both sides. The managers who mediated the conflicts could then transfer the worker to another crew if they could not work out their differences. Looking into the conflict to help the foreman and worker solve the problem builds loyalty and increases safety on the job. It creates a "win-win" situation. From the foreman's point of view, the conflict is either resolved and they both feel comfortable about working together again or the worker is removed from the crew. The worker either continues in a situation which is now comfortable or has an opportunity to move to another crew; neither of these solutions is as threatening as being fired.

The effect of the constructive ways of handling personnel problems that are described in this chapter must surely reach beyond the individuals directly involved to the entire job-site workforce to reduce job tensions. We all know that we may make mistakes on our jobs. We each then try to predict how our boss will handle it. Will we be treated drastically, perhaps be fired, or will we be given an opportunity to learn from the mistake and continue to contribute to the project? A single example of firing can spread a fear of drastic treatment through a workforce, creating widespread tensions. Such tensions among the workers have been shown to produce a greater likelihood of accidents.

Rewarding for Good Work

How managers handle situations in which subordinates do an excellent job can also affect safety performance. Safer crews were more likely to state that their managers praised them for doing a good job (Samelson, 1983). They were careful to point out, however, that indiscriminate praise, without a good basis in fact was counterproductive. Recognizing when subordinates do an excellent job can be a real morale booster, increasing liking for the job and decreasing feelings of pressure. Certainly well-deserved praise is an inexpensive and effective means for building people's skills, self-confidence, and desire to be productive.

Dangers of Using Competition and Pressure

There are two methods of motivating workers which have side effects detrimental to job safety: competition and pressure for productivity.

Hinze asked his sample of job-site managers, "If you have two crews doing the same type of work, such as forming up a 10-foot wall, do you think it is a good idea to try to get them to compete?"

The managers who answered No to this question, who did *not* rely on competition to increase productivity, had the safer records (Hinze, 1976). Using competition as a primary motivating tool can encourage people to take unsafe shortcuts; it can also increase emotional tensions.

The job-site managers who avoid using techniques which may pressure people so that they ignore safety in their hurry to complete the work have the safer records. Hinze also found, for example, that those job-site managers who used cost information to put pressure on the workers had a higher average injury frequency than those who did not use cost information in this way. Since the job-site managers rated as excellent by their superiors on their ability to meet costs had significantly few injuries on their jobs than those rated less positively, using cost information to pressure workers may well be counterproductive not only for safety but also for meeting costs.

Maintaining Employment Continuity

Another indication of job-site managers' long-run interest in their workforce is the proportion of their workers that has worked for them on previous jobs. This continuity of employment does not come about automatically. Managers with excellent safety records spend time and energy to maintain contact with their good workers.

A job-site manager who lives and works in the California Sierras where most construction is seasonal obtained a contract for snow removal to keep the best foremen working through the winter months. Furthermore, to keep in touch through the winter with the other workers and foremen who have worked for him, he goes out to dinner with all those living in the area once a month.

In Hinze's sample of managers, he found that those who rehire 50 percent or more of their workers have far fewer accidents on their jobs than those who rehire fewer than 50 percent.

The research results already presented help us to understand why a workforce might be interested in working again for the same job-site manager. The managers with the safer records have better methods for handling such basic questions as motivating the workforce, hirings, layoffs, and firings and for handling job successes and failures. As we have seen in this chapter those who do not permit foremen to fire crew members and those who seldom use firing themselves to "solve" personnel problems have better records than those who rely more on firing.

Managers with such constructive ways of handling people problems are ones for whom foremen and workers would like to work again.

How continuity of employment decreases accidents

There are several reasons why having this continuity with a large proportion of the workers helps managers on job safety. First there are many people on their new projects who have already been trained by them and know their priorities and approaches to problems. These workers can form a nucleus to help train others. A job starting with half or more of the people having worked with the project manager reduces the size of but not the necessity for orientation. All of the employees will of course need orientation to the new project, but many of them already know in part what to expect and what is expected of them. Also many of them have already formed working relationships with each other; these increase their ability to cooperate and reduce tensions between them.

This manpower continuity may also be an indirect indication of the effectivenss in handling people of the managers with the better safety records. Since in most cases workers laid off from one job can find work with a number of other project managers, the managers who can attract more of their trained and competent workforce back to their next job gain from their past good working relationships.

These results taken together indicate that those job-site managers who have long-range people building as one of their major goals are likely to develop a more loyal and safer workforce.

Summary

- Consider your workforce, both salaried and hourly, as your most important resource. Build long-run commitment and loyalty so that training now can pay off for the future.

- Manage now so that the workers on your present project will want to be hired on your next one.

- Recognize subordinates, including work crews, who do an excellent job.

- Develop options to firing so that firing is a last resort.

- Listen to both sides in a foreman-worker conflict.

- Avoid using methods, such as competition between crews, which may pressure workers and encourage them to take unsafe shortcuts.

14

Summary of Action Steps for Job-Site Managers

Job safety management can be divided into five major areas: (1) setting priorities on the job, (2) planning for safe construction, (3) orienting workers, (4) maintaining the communications safety net, and (5) people building.

Priorities

1. Commit yourself to the combined goal of high safety and high productivity.
2. Include money for safety equipment and safety personnel into the project budget.
3. Begin communicating your productivity and safety goal to owners, subcontractors, and union representatives in prejob meetings.
4. Make safety rules and regulations an integrated part of job rules.
5. In new-worker orientation include job rules, make it clear that infractions of them are cause for termination.
6. Train your superintendents and foremen to review job exposures as work progresses and revise job procedures to keep work safe.
7. Use toolbox meetings and on-the-job training to maintain safe, productive job procedures.
8. Show your commitment to keeping the job safe by:
   a. Walking the job with safety eyes.
   b. Monitoring the job for housekeeping, OSHA requirements, and other unsafe conditions and acts.
   c. Working cooperatively with job safety people and letting project personnel know that the safety people represent you.

   d. Enforcing standards for safe behavior at all times.
   e. Monitoring subcontractors.

Planning

1. Take the time to plan; it will reduce costs, improve the job schedule, and benefit safety by decreasing hazards and job pressures.
2. Before the job starts:
   a. Review cost estimates and schedules and, if necessary, negotiate revisions to avoid stress and the temptation to take hazardous shortcuts later.
   b. Work with the safety people to develop a safety plan for the life of the project.
   c. Gain cooperation and input from key people in prejob discussions: on union jobs, from union representatives; on highly hazardous jobs, from representatives from the consultation service of the OSHA program.
3. Maintain three levels of planning throughout the project: large scale, weekly, and daily and include safety in all levels of planning.
4. Discuss safety in daily planning meetings and weekly job schedule and progress meetings.
5. Remember that last minute changes of plans are often dangerous—caution supervisors and workers against them.

Worker Orientation

1. To keep accidents from happening, require job and project orientation for all new hires no matter how long their years of experience in their work or with the company and no matter how short their stay on the project will be.
2. Welcome each new worker if at all possible.
3. For company and general project orientation consider a short slide-tape or video presentation introduced by a job-site management representative.
4. For job-site orientation include a short site tour; on large projects develop a site map that shows the overall layout of the project with a short description of the project stages.
5. Delegate detailed orientation to the worker's foreman, making sure that foremen are trained to conduct effective new-worker orientation, including explaining specific safe and productive job procedures rather than talking in vague generalities about being safe.

6. On projects or parts of projects with high potential for accidents require orientation before each new phase of the work.

Effective Communication

1. Expand your communication system beyond the chain of command to include direct contact with workers and group meetings. Train your management team to expect you to use these other methods for information.

2. Walk the job each day, talk to craft workers, bring your safety commitment to them, hear their suggestions, and report actions taken.

3. Meet with supervisory groups on a regular basis; meet with groups of foremen and craft workers for planning and feedback.

4. Develop toolbox meetings as a valuable information and training tool, attend meetings yourself on a rotating basis, and train foremen to keep to job-specific topics.

5. On home office communication—keep them informed daily; do not pass on to your project management team and workers pressures from the home office.

People Building

1. Before every action and decision of yours, ask yourself the question, "How will this affect my work force?" Your most important resource is your people. Manage now to achieve their long-run commitment and loyalty.

2. Listen to both sides in conflicts, for example, in those between foremen and workers, rather than automatically backing the superior.

3. Develop other options than firing—firing is usually a poor way to handle a problem; do not delegate that power to subordinates.

4. Thank supervisors and craft workers when they do excellent work.

The Foreman

Construction foremen have tough, challenging jobs. They are the vital links in the construction process, serving where the blueprints are transformed into actions that result in buildings, dams, highways, and homes. The plans are just pieces of paper until they are changed at the foreman level into parts of the built environment. Foremen directing their crews are therefore the backbone of the construction industry.

By foreman we mean the first-line supervisor, the man or woman who directs the workers. On a large project, there will be a number of craft foremen supervising their crews. Very small contractors running their work out of their pickup trucks who organize, plan, and supervise the workers themselves are foremen by our definition, as well as being the CEOs and job-site managers.

The foremen are the ones who present safety to the workers on an hour-by-hour, day-by-day basis. They are helped a great deal if both the company and the job-site manager do their share in safety management. But no matter how good the company's program and how committed the job-site manager, a very important part of a total safety program is lost if the foremen do not bring safety into the job as a regular part of the work.

*In other words: **no other supervisors can take the place of the foremen directing their crews by using methods which keep accidents from happening.***

In a study entitled: The Effect of Foremen on Safety in Construction *(Samelson, 1977) foremen were interviewed on how they handled their jobs. They were also measured on their crew safety record and on four other areas of job performance: (1) ability to meet costs, (2) productivity level, (3) ability to work under pressure, and (4) administrative ability. The results of this research indicated a number of ways in which foremen can affect the safety and productivity of their crews. Other data on the impact of foremen on safety comes from a study of crew factors (Samelson, 1983).*

Knowing what the safe, productive foremen do differently from the less safe and less productive foremen makes it possible to provide foremen with methods of working with their crews which will improve both productivity and safety. The chapters in this section will describe these effective foremen methods.

Highly productive foremen with excellent safety records not only have special methods and techniques for achieving their goals with their crews, but they also believe in two essential principles of safety management: **Construction safety management at the crew level is (1) very important and (2) very practical and achievable.**

Stated differently, these foremen consider themselves **accountable** *for safety right along with productivity and quality and they* **have developed methods** *for achieving the goal of eliminating accidents in their crews. The methods they use will be described in the next four chapters.*

We will include in these chapters excerpts from in-depth interviews (from the foreman study) with two highly safe foremen who are called Bill Hartmann and Mike Stella—to protect their privacy. Bill Hartmann, a labor foreman, has supervised crews for 19 years without a lost-time accident. Mike Stella, an operating engineer foreman, at last report had gone 200,000 man-hours with no disabling injury to any crew member. These excerpts show in detail how very safe and productive foremen supervise their crews.

15

Starting New Workers Out Right

The most important single difference between the foremen with the very safe crews and those whose crews have more accidents is in the handling of new workers. Furthermore, statistics show that the first days and weeks on the job are the times when most accidents occur if new workers are not given the right start. Attention to the new worker, therefore, is essential for all foremen who want to keep their crews from being hurt.

The foremen with the excellent safety records consider everyone who joins the crew a new worker—regardless of their prior experience in the craft or with the company and regardless of how short their stay may be on the site.

These foremen spend time orienting each of their new workers even though they recognize that these workers were hired because they were needed immediately. Although the time pressures might tempt them to cut corners, they know that putting new workers to work at once—even those highly experienced in their craft—will lead to costly delays, mistakes, and even accidents. The safer, more productive foremen save money and time in the long run by starting new workers out slowly at the beginning.

Orientation for everyone is essential because each construction project is a new hazardous environment, one that is changing constantly throughout the life of the project.

Steps in New-Worker Orientation

We can summarize how the foremen with excellent safety records handle new-worker orientation by listing their action steps:

Ask about the last job. By keeping the questions specific, foremen can get answers which help them get to know the new workers and find out their past experience in detail. This information guides the foremen in deciding initial job assignment and possible supplementary on-the-job training.

Describe the new job and the job rules. Right from the beginning, the safe, productive foremen make clear that safety is an integral part of their work rules. They believe in one way of working, "the safe productive way," and they make sure that each new worker understands this from the start.

Give worker a test run on equipment and/or tools.

Mike Stella, an excavation foreman with an excellent safety record, assigns each new operating engineer a job of moving dirt in a safe place that is easy to observe from his pickup truck. The new worker, without realizing it, is being given a test run. New workers who handle the equipment successfully on the small test job are then ready for the next stage of Mike Stella's orientation: a tour of the site to show where the work will be carried out.

Many construction companies could take a tip from Mike Stella's approach to new employees and thus make sure that their expensive equipment is being operated by knowledgeable, skilled personnel.

Big W Construction Company top executives realized that handing over equipment worth hundreds of thousands of dollars to untried employees was not only unsafe but also very costly. They therefore had their equipment manufacturers make dual-operated models of each of their major pieces of equipment. Each new operator first goes out on training runs on this dual-operation equipment with an instructor. The new employee is then tested before being permitted to operate the standard equipment.

Dual-operated equipment is not always a practical solution, however, so each foreman needs to think through the best way to test workers on their ability to use the tools or equipment which they will be operating in their work.

Show worker around site. A tour of the whole site may already have been given the new worker by job management. If not, the foreman should take the new worker on such a tour. It not only gives the foreman an opportunity to point out the layout and major job hazards, but it also allows the two of them to get to know each other a little better.

Start new crew members out slowly. The highly safe productive foreman pays a great deal of attention to new employees and starts them out very slowly on the job.

> Bill Hartmann, a labor foreman with 19 years of supervising crews without a lost-time accident, does not let the new employee do anything but watch the crew the first day.

Watch out for the new worker for the first few days. The foremen with excellent productivity and safety records were more watchful of the new workers. There are a number of reasons why being watchful helps both productivity and safety.

One of the first aims of these outstanding foremen is to create a direct line of communication between themselves and the new worker. They want to ensure that their priorities and rules will be the ones which determine the way the new worker tackles the job; they also want to give the new crew member a means for asking questions; and they realize that getting questions answered can reduce the tensions related to beginning a new job.

Involve the crew in watching out for the new worker. The foreman also can and should involve the other crew members in the job of watching out for the new worker. Crews with safer records make a point of watching out for new members (Samelson, 1983). Such concern for the new workers decreases accidents. New employees cannot know the particular dangers of the site and project they have just come onto. Therefore, only from others can they learn what acts are unsafe and what conditions are dangerous.

New-Crew Orientation

At the beginning of the job, foremen have entire crews of new workers even though some of the workers may have worked for their foremen before. The initial meeting with a new crew is very crucial since it sets the stage for what is to come. The new crew members are eager to find out what their priorities should be and what is going to make a difference on the job, i.e., what basis the foreman will use to decide when and whether they are doing a good job.

The foremen with excellent safety and productivity records gather the crew together right at the start. They make clear that they require safe, productive work. For foremen in companies with job management and top management support for safety, as well as productivity, there may be no need to state their priorities in the extreme form which Bill Hartmann, a labor foreman with 25 years of experience, describes. (At the time he was interviewed, he was working for a company that had virtually no awareness of the values of safety.)

At the start of a job I get the crew together and tell them what I expect of them. (I use words that aren't in the dictionary.) I tell them just what I expect of them and I tell them if they don't want to do that they had better step right up now and I will pay them for their first two hours and they can go back to the hall now. They can decide. If they don't work, they will go. I let them know that if I didn't do that, I would go.

Hartmann expects his workers to work safely. If someone does something unsafe it will be: "One warning and then they go. With this federal law [OSHA], if a worker were killed I would be behind bars on a manslaughter charge. I let them know I'm not going to take chances."

Many foremen have the authority to hire crew members but, unlike Bill Hartmann, cannot fire them without the involvement of their job-site manager. Under such circumstances, foremen can state to their new crew that they do not tolerate unsafe acts, that they will have any worker who does not work safely removed from their crew. Such a statement underlines their requirement that crew members work productively and safely at all times. Foremen with outstanding safety records realize that at least some of their new crew members may have been working last for a company which only paid lip service to safety; their message must be clear and unambiguous.

Orienting the Crew throughout the Job

Foremen with excellent safety records also gather the crew together *whenever* there is a need to repeat the rules and priorities.

Mike Stella travels around in his pickup truck watching the crew working the equipment. If there is a near miss, he immediately pulls everyone off their equipment for a safety meeting.

Toolbox meetings on a weekly basis are also useful for involving the crew in planning ahead for safe, productive work and for looking back to see ways to improve. These meetings should be used for weekly crew orientation rather than treating them as a routine requirement. Details on how to make toolbox meetings effective are included in Chapter 17, "Training for Safety."

Summary

Starting new workers out right is the single most important task for foremen who want to keep their crew members safe.

New-worker orientation

How safe, productive foremen orient their new workers can be summarized in the following guidelines for foremen:

1. Ask about the last job.
2. Describe the new job and your specific rules that combine work and safety.
3. Give worker a test run on equipment and/or tools.
4. Show worker around site.
5. Introduce workers to other crew members.
6. Start new crew members out slowly.
7. Keep an eye on the new worker during the first few days.
8. Encourage crew members to watch out for their new member.

New-crew orientation

- At your first meeting with your crew tell them that you require them to work safely at all times.
- Stop work and bring your whole crew together whenever there are changes in the work requirements or there is a near miss.
- Use weekly toolbox meetings for planning ahead to keep the work safe and productive.

16

Working with Crews

The Mike Stellas and the Bill Hartmanns—the highly effective foremen in both productivity and safety—not only do more crew-member orientation, they also have a whole set of special methods for working with their crews.

The excellent foremen know that a foreman has to lead others. Even though crew members are members of the same union or craft and one or more of them may even have been foremen on other jobs, a foreman cannot just be "one of the gang." The job requires playing a special role: carrying the responsibility for supervising the crew and organizing and planning the work.

The highly effective foremen also know how to handle other complexities of the foreman's role. Foremen are the first-line supervisors of the construction industry yet, as foremen, they typically have no security or seniority. Their position usually does not last beyond a specific project. For the next job they must be rehired. On that next job they may become foremen again or may instead be skilled craftsmen working under other foremen. Quoting from the interview with Mike Stella again:

> When the job finished on which Mike Stella had been foreman, he was put on another job as a worker. The foreman was young and reluctant to tell Mike, who was older and had many years of experience as a foreman, what to do. Mike then explained that the person who has been named foreman has to act like it. He told the young foreman that the foremen are the ones who will be blamed if things go wrong, so they need to take responsibility [for leadership].

The methods of outstanding foremen are highlighted by seeing how they handle typical situations on the job such as: (1) their crews turning out less work than expected, (2) job crises, (3) crews doing an excellent job, (4) finding a risk taker in the crew, (5) having a crew member with home problems, and (6) choosing crews and crew members.

Handling Low Crew Productivity

When the crew is not turning out the work that they should, a typical reaction is to start putting pressure on them. But putting pressure on the crew is not the most effective way to bring about an improvement in the work, and it also increases the chances for accidents. *A much more effective method to achieve high performance from the crew is to analyze the problem.*

The foreman with a productivity problem who can keep from telling the crew that they need to turn out more work and can instead start looking at exactly *why* the workers are not getting more work done will have a much more productive and safer crew. By focusing on how to solve the problem, rather than blaming the crew for the low productivity, the foreman and the crew can work together on solving it. Crews see such foremen as very perceptive and helpful and want to do a good job for them.

Foremen whose answer to low productivity is to pressure the crew build tensions and negativism in them; they make their crews feel that they are more of a hindrance than a help. The crews of such foremen have lower productivity and poorer safety performance.

Problem analysis rather than pressuring the crew pays off for the foreman! Suggested action steps for foremen are:

1. Consider what you can do to help your crew do their job.

2. Ask them what they need in order to do their work.

3. Use planning so that pressuring the crew is avoided.

Handling Crises

Foremen who can keep cool even when there are all kinds of snafus on the job will have higher productivity and better safety performance in their crews. The way foremen react to job crises, particularly the extent to which they become angry at their crews, is of central importance to safety and to productivity as well.

The high productivity, high safety foremen have a number of methods to keep themselves even tempered despite job frustrations.

> Mike Stella does not vent his anger on his crew. If he is angry, he goes off a little way from the crew to cool down a bit before talking to a crew member. He says he stays cool and keeps his temper because otherwise the crew member will just want to get back at him.

Cooling off rather than sounding off makes it easier to analyze problems, and it keeps anger from spreading on the job. As Stella points out, anger breeds anger and vindictiveness. Foremen who lose their tempers at one of their workers can turn that worker against them and the goals for which they are working. Furthermore, anger creates tensions in people, making them forget the hazards and dangers of the job. It also can easily lead to taking chances. For these reasons, it is apparent that uncontrolled anger increases the likelihood of accidents.

Responding to Good Work

Question: What should a foreman do if a crew turns out a very good job?

Answer: Thank them for a job well done.

Praising good work sounds like an easy way to improve productivity, safety, and morale. And it is easy once you have become used to doing it. The foremen who have learned how to notice good work and extra effort have highly productive and safe crews; they keep watching for success; and whenever they can, they tell their crews that they are doing an excellent job.

Crew members tell us that their foreman's praise must be deserved to be meaningful. A foreman who does not know good work from bad cannot of course give praise for good work. A routine pat on the back is not what the highly effective foremen do. Their thanks are deserved and genuine.

The stereotype of the construction foreman who only swears at the crew is far from the truth; the success of the excellent construction foremen demonstrates that a word of well-deserved praise is a much more likely occurrence among outstanding foremen.

Handling the Risk Taker

The foremen who achieve the better safety records consider that they are responsible for eliminating unsafe acts among their crew members. To follow through on this responsibility they make very clear to their workers that unsafe behavior is not allowed on the job. Any unsafe behavior is stopped immediately. Taking risks on the job is not acceptable.

> Mike Stella, the outstanding equipment operator foreman, listens to the way his operators drive. Good steady driving is fine, but if one operator begins to "hot-rod" the equipment or do anything else unsafe, Mike immediately flags the operator down and tells him to stop; otherwise the crew members would challenge each other until they were all driving wildly.

Stopping unsafe acts right away keeps them from building up. If one member is allowed to get away with working unsafely, others follow, and soon the whole crew will be taking risks. Unsafe behavior escalates quickly.

By observing crew members for unsafe acts and taking immediate action to correct them, foremen not only keep unsafe acts from spreading through a crew, but they also begin to build a safety consciousness among their crew members. Very safe crews watch out for each other and stop each other when they see one of their members doing something unsafe (Samelson, 1983).

Keeping Home Tensions off the Job

One of the questions that every foreman has to face is how to treat the worker who has personal problems. Should the foreman make time to be a sympathetic listener for off-the-job problems? The foremen with the excellent safety records would say: "No, a foreman trying to be a psychologist will only mess up the job." Instead, their only connection with the personal problems of their crew members is to grant them time off when they need it. Talking about personal and home life fears and worries on the job is evidently more likely to simply activate these fears and worries in the work situation. In the foreman study this result is stated as follows:

> Again and again the safe foremen told of their philosophy for themselves and their crew that the job needs everyone's full attention; this means dealing only with work problems at work and leaving home problems at home (Samelson, 1977)

Keeping Attention Focused on the Job

There is an underlying fact behind the methods that excellent foremen use to handle the problems of low productivity, job crises, and off-the-job personal and family concerns. Keeping cool and not losing one's temper, analyzing problems rather than pressuring the crew, keeping home problems off the job—each of these methods produces a calm job atmosphere rather than a tense, emotional one. *A calm job atmosphere contributes strongly to an excellent safety record. Tension, anger, fear, and worry on the job are conducive to accidents.*

We will need more research to determine exactly why anger, fear, and worry increase accidents and why reducing such emotions on the job keeps workers safer. We do, however, have some good hunches. Anger, fear, worries—these emotions turn the worker's attention inward; thus the worker does not stay alert to the dangers which are ever-present on the construction site. In the foreman study this effect was called *sense blocking* to indicate that the worker evidently does not perceive or is less alert to the environment when preoccupied with worries, fears, or anger.

It is a proven fact, however, that any conditions which reduce a worker's attention to the construction environment have the potential for increasing accidents. Excellent foremen handle problems with crew members in ways to keep attention focused on the job and away from personal problems and worries.

Their awareness of the importance of attention also leads them to be watchful for any signs of preoccupation in their crew members.

Handling Vulnerable Workers

There are a number of conditions which reduce attention and thus a worker's ability to behave safely in the construction environment. After deciding that a worker is too preoccupied or is behaving erratically, the foreman first chooses a course of action to protect both the worker and others form being hurt. For some temporary conditions, all that the worker may need is a rest period or a job reassignment.

> Mike Stella not only watches out for the new worker and the one back at work after being off, but he also keeps a special eye out for crew members who appear to be less alert than usual. After watching such a worker, he may decide to talk the worker into going home again. Or he may feel that the condition is not serious enough for that and may, instead, reassign the worker to less demanding work or ask the other crew members to watch out for him.

Drugs and alcohol are two factors which can seriously impair an individual's ability to pay attention; they also can affect motor coordination and control. Workers on construction sites under the influence of either drugs or alcohol are dangerous to themselves and others; therefore very safe foremen are always on the look out for any signs of such workers.

> Bill Hartmann has this to say about drinking: "I'm not against drinking. I like to get together with the crew after work, but if I smell liquor on anyone's breath on the job, they go home with a warning the first time and then they go out."

As we have mentioned previously, Bill Hartmann has to handle all safety problems himself without any help from his company. In many companies that have a commitment to safety, foremen can discuss with their safety representatives what can be for workers with drug or alcohol problems—other than not allowing them to work in situations in which they could hurt themselves or others. Often communities have rehabilitation centers that workers can be referred to for evaluation and treatment.

Maintaining a Continuity of Experience

Foremen with excellent safety and productivity records know how important it is to have some crew members who have worked with them previously. Having crew members with experience with the work, with the foreman, and with each other means that not everyone has as much to learn on the new project. It means too that what the new workers learn from the foreman is supported by the actions and attitudes of experienced crew members. This continuity of experience helps reduce accidents.

In our discussion of new workers, we stressed the value of the foreman getting to know the new workers and watching out for them during their first few days. Very experienced and well-trained workers on a crew can provide extra help in watching out for the new workers and can help too with on-the-job training.

In the section on job-site managers we discussed the importance to managers of staffing a new job with many workers who have been with them before. Effective job-site managers rely on foremen with whom they have worked before. These foremen in turn contact workers they knew from previous jobs for their crews on the new job.

> In talking about his present job and future possibilities, Bill Hartmann told how he hoped that the company with an excellent safety record for which he had worked before would be the successful bidder on a job near his home. "If I got a call from them right now, I could get on the phone and line up a crew and be ready tomorrow." He keeps in touch by Christmas cards with many of those who have worked for him in the past and has a book with their addresses and telephone numbers ready.

This example illustrates the loyalty which workers have toward foremen who are committed to safety. It also illustrates the loyalty which a company with an outstanding safety record creates in its foremen. The foremen whose crews want to work with them again are excellent in helping their crews be both safe and productive. And by working together on job after job these teams of workers and foremen become even safer and more productive.

Maintaining Crew Friendliness

One worthwhile question about forming crews is, "Should friends work together or not?" Supervisors often fear that friends will spend too much of their time socializing and will be less productive and safe. There is no evidence to justify this fear. In fact, the limited research shows that crews made up of buddies are more productive and safer. A study of safer crews found that they were more likely to have people in them who were friends outside work (Samelson, 1983). Friends are more likely to look out for each other. We all have our off days and sometimes need to be reminded to wear protective equipment, watch out for hazards, etc. Friends will remind us to protect ourselves.

Planning for the Crew

One of the most important parts of the foreman's job is crew planning. Planning helps increase crew safety through decreasing pressures and tensions and through providing an opportunity to choose the safest and most efficient methods. There are some general guidelines to planning even though each craft has unique types of activities.

Basically planning permits job decisions to be made with consideration of the many factors involved. Foremen have to make many job decisions. For example they may have to select:

- The size of crew and members for particular tasks
- The order in which different jobs should be done
- The time and place to use special equipment
- The tool and materials storage locations
- Housekeeping methods and times

Each of these types of decisions affect safety; each requires planning. If a foreman fails to think ahead, the decisions will be made without considering which alternative would be best to meet the goal of safe, productive work.

Materials handling

The safe productive foremen pay special attention to the handling of materials. These foremen plan materials storage in order to eliminate complicated and difficult moving; they store the materials neatly and close to the usage points. Such preplanned storage will decrease both the potential for accidents and costly delays when small loads must be transported by workers to the work point. The longer and more complicated the route that workers must take to move materials from the storage location to the place where they will actually be used, the greater the possibility of accidents and of time wasted. Planning materials placement then is one of the ways in which a foreman can speed up a job and increase safety. It is clear that storage and placement of materials needs close attention by the foreman.

Observation of jobs has shown, however, that often there is no planning involved in choosing the temporary locations for materials. The driver of the truck delivering the materials simply dumps them in an empty place convenient for the driver. Letting the selection of a materials storage place just happen is likely to mean that the place is poorly located for both convenience and safety. The foreman can, however, plan ahead to avoid such built-in inefficiencies and make clear to all relevant people where delivered materials should be left.

Another important part of planning for effective materials handling involves deciding on the size and weight of loads workers should be permitted to carry. Awkward sizes and heavy loads put undue strains on backs. Furthermore, a size or weight which could be safely carried by a worker for a single time can create back injuries if it is repeated many times. By planning crew work and assigning two people to awkward and heavier loads, foreman can reduce back injuries, the most frequent cause of long-term disability in construction.

Housekeeping

Planning for effective housekeeping is one of the easiest ways to improve productivity and safety. Not clearing up as the job moves along soon creates an obstacle course that is not only unsafe but also requires so much side stepping and detouring that it slows the work down a great deal. Hammering nails down is another task that should be done as the work progresses. Before the end of the shift, lumber should be cleaned or stripped of nails for reuse and scrap lumber discarded. The job area needs to be clean and clear for the start of the next work day.

Developing checklists

One method for foremen to help themselves organize their jobs is to develop checklists of jobs needing to be done, etc. Figure 16.1 illustrates such a checklist for roofer foremen which is attached to each job-order form. A checklist, however, does not need to be printed to be useful; it does need to be made in multiple copies, however.

ROOFING
Foreman Safety Checklist

Emergency Phone Numbers

_____

_____

Nearest hospital or clinic

_____

ADDRESS

Roof readiness   ☐ clean
    ☐ openings barricaded
    ☐ perimeter protected
☐ Materials handling planned
☐ Proper equipment in working order
☐ Crew clothed in hard hats, safety
    shoes, long sleeves

☐ Workers fit physically and mentally
☐ Special attention given to new workers
☐ First aid kits stocked and accessible
☐ Fire extinguishers available
    and operative
☐ Water available for drinking and burns
☐ Weather conditions deserving
    attention
    ☐ wind
    ☐ heat
    ☐ slippery deck

Special instructions _____

_____

_____

_____

_____

Developed by Construction Safety, Civil Engineering, Stanford University, CA 94305

Figure 16.1 Roofing foreman safety checklist.

Summary

- When your crew is not accomplishing as much as expected, analyze the problem rather than telling them to do more, putting pressure on them, or not doing anything.

- When anyone makes you angry, first cool off and then handle the problem calmly rather than getting mad at crew members.

- Praise good safe work.

- Stop unsafe acts immediately.

- Keep home tensions off the job. Do not discuss personal problems at work. Send workers with problems home or to a source of help.

- Build loyalty among your crew members so that you can count on them on this job and on your next one.

- Encourage friends to work together.

- Plan your work including materials handling and housekeeping.

17

Foreman Training

Construction companies with safer records understand the key importance of foremen follow through for safety. They know that foremen training is well worth the effort. They realize that such training helps to make their foremen members of the management team. The training investment pays off in foremen competence and in foremen loyalty to the company. In the top management study, Levitt found that companies which had special orientation programs for newly hired or promoted foremen had experience modification rates 29 percent lower on the average than companies which did not (Levitt, 1975, p. 76).

Traditionally it has been hard to convince contractors to spend time and money on training their foremen. Construction foremen are almost never salaried employees of the company and yet they are functionally a part of management. If the workforce is unionized, the foremen are members of the union, usually of the same union as their crew. Yet if they are to do their jobs well, they must also consider themselves members of management and be considered as such by management.

Foreman training, therefore, is a very integral part of effective construction management. Our research indicates that it increases loyalty to the company and also improves safety performance.

Foremen can improve their safety record through attending courses which teach basic principles of safety management. Some large companies develop their own courses. Other companies join together to support such mutually beneficial training. We shall use as an example one such jointly sponsored course: the Laborer's-AGC Line Foreman Safety Training Course.

Laborer's-AGC Line Foreman Safety Training Course

This safety training course for foremen is given under the auspices of the Laborer's-AGC Education and Training Fund, a fund jointly sponsored and administered by the Laborer's International Union of North America and the Associated General Contractors of America. In an evaluation of this training course (Levitt et al., 1984), the course was rated as very effective by attendees in:

1. Teaching them how to observe people for unsafe acts
2. Convincing them that safety should be equal to production, morale, quality, and cost in their work
3. Making them feel responsible for eliminating unsafe acts and hazards from their work situation
4. Convincing them to make a commitment to safety in their job
5. Teaching them how to recognize hazards on construction sites

This course covers a number of areas of importance for supervising crews for excellent safety performance. Some important topics, however, were not covered by this course at the time it was studied and should be part of an expanded foreman training program. They include worker and crew orientation, job planning, handling low productivity, keeping cool on the job, rewarding good work, handling home tensions, and maintaining crew continuity and friendliness. Another needed area is training in spotting and handling workers with drug or alcohol problems.

Running Effective Toolbox Meetings

Toolbox or tailgate meetings are very often the foreman's responsibility, yet it is rare for anyone to give a foreman training on how to run a good meeting. These meetings, however, can be a valuable way to plan and carry out safe, productive work; they do not have to be boring and ineffective. Here are some relatively easy methods which foremen can use to do a better job conducting toolbox meetings:

1. Before the meeting
   a. Pick a single problem or hazard which you feel is particularly relevant to the upcoming work.
   b. Consider ways to control this hazard

2. At the meeting
   a. Where possible bring an object which relates to the problem or

**Suggested
Tailgate Meeting Topics
in Underground Construction**

- Cave-in prevention and protection
- Positive ventilation in confined space
- Overhead high voltage lines
- Traffic control
- Pipelaying
- Trenching
- Earthmoving equipment
- Rolling pipe
- Water mains and utilities in trench or area
- First aid and emergency telephone numbers
- Power tools
- Effects of equipment vibration on trenches
- Personal protective equipment
- Poisonous plants: poison oak, etc.
- Pacing work and lifting techniques
- Housekeeping

Developed by Stanford University Civil Engineering Construction Safety and Health Project, Stanford, CA 94305   (415) 497-4447

**Suggestions
for Tailgate Meetings
in Underground Construction**

Before the meeting
- Pick a single hazard which you feel is particularly relevant to the upcoming work.
- Consider ways to control this hazard. (Additional ideas might be found in Cal/Osha guide)

At the meeting
- Tell your workers the hazard to be discussed at today's meeting and give an example from your own experience.
- Ask workers by name for their suggestions of what the hazards are and how they might be controlled.
- Summarize what has been said and add your input.
- Encourage your workers to ask questions.
- Keep meetings brief (5-10 minutes).

This material was prepared under grant number EJFOD342 from the Occupational Safety and Health Administration, U.S. Department of Labor. Points of view or opinions stated in this document do not necessarily reflect the views or policies of the U.S. Department of Labor.

SF0880

Figure 17.1 Pocket card for foremen in underground construction.

hazard (rusty nail, hammer with splayed head, a recent picture of crew's housekeeping problem, etc.) to get their attention.

b. Tell your workers the problem or hazard to be discussed at today's meeting and give an example from your own experience.
c. Ask workers by name for their suggestions on how to solve the problem and reduce the risks.
d. Summarize what has been said and add your input.
e. Keep meetings brief (about 10 minutes).

In order to be ready for toolbox meetings, foremen should prepare a list of areas which might make good topics. Figure 17.1 shows such a list for underground construction.

Foremen can gain training in how to speak effectively by joining local community groups for improving speaking and leadership ability, such as Toastmasters.

Spotting Safety Violations versus Supervising Safely

Some safety training programs concentrate almost entirely on teaching foremen how to spot safety violations. If training programs limit themselves just to the area of improving a foreman's ability to see safety violations, the improvements in crew safety may well be minimal. In the foreman study this question was investigated: Are the foremen with the best ability to spot safety violations the ones with the best crew safety records? When foremen were given pictures of job sites with safety violations, it was found that *there was no relationship between ability to correctly identify safety violations and crew safety record* (Samelson, 1977).

This result means that it is not enough for foremen to learn as much as they can about federal and state safety standards. As we have seen from the preceding parts of this section, supervising a crew safely requires a number of skills in handling workers. The only way for a foreman to be sure that the crew will have an excellent safety record is to adopt the supervisory methods which safe foremen use to make their crew members work safely.

According to another result from the foremen study, the foremen with the safer records do have a more favorable attitude toward the Occupational Safety and Health Act (OSHA) than the foremen with the poorer records. The safer foremen are more likely to believe that complying with OSHA standards has not increased their costs.

Understanding federal and state safety standards, therefore, is an important part of foreman training when it is combined with training in how to orient new workers, how to work with crews, and how to plan the work.

Summary of Action Steps for Foremen

Foremen are the keys to construction safety and productivity. Research results show that there is no need for safety versus productivity trade-offs; foreman can and many do obtain safe, productive performance from their crews.

Highly productive foremen with excellent safety records prove that safety management at the crew level is practical and achievable. Their special methods and techniques for working with their crews fall into two main categories: new-worker orientation and working with crews. They also recognize the need in themselves for training for safety.

Starting New Workers Out Right

New-worker orientation

If foremen could only do one thing to improve their crew's safety record, the choice is clear: *Concentrate on orienting the new workers.*

New workers include everyone new to the crew—no matter how experienced. The most important things to do with each new crew member are listed in the following steps:

- Ask specific questions about the last job to find out experience.
- Describe the new job and its rules, which include safety.
- Give worker a test run on appropriate equipment and/or tools.
- Show worker around site if job management did not.
- Introduce worker to other crew members.
- Start new worker out slowly by first just watching.

- Watch out for new workers during first few days; check back on them.
- Encourage crew members to watch out for their new member.

New-crew orientation

- When a new job starts, meet with your new crew immediately.
- Make it clear to the crew that you require everyone to work safely and productively at all times.
- Describe your job rules (safe, effective procedures).
- Give crew members test runs on equipment and/or tools.
- Conduct a site tour (if this has not been done already)
- Meet with the new crew every few days for further orientation, questions from them, discussion, etc.

Orienting the crew throughout the job

- Gather your crew together whenever you need to discuss rules, priorities, and work procedures; for example, after a near miss or before starting a new part of the job.
- Use weekly toolbox meetings to plan safety and productivity improvements.

Working with Crews

Foremen have the responsibility to lead their crews. Guidelines for effective crew leadership include:

- When your crew turns out less work than is expected, analyze the problem; find out why crew productivity is low. Avoid telling them to work harder or faster.
- Keep your cool during job crises—getting mad at your crew can lead to accidents.
- Notice and praise excellent work by crew members.
- Immediately stop any crew member who is doing something unsafe.
- Give workers time off for personal problems; do not try to discuss their problems with them on the job.
- Be on the look out for decreased attention or poor motor coordination in your crew. Do not permit such workers to operate equipment or to work in situations in which they could hurt themselves or others. Either reassign them, send them home, or refer them to help.

- Treat your crew members with respect so that they will want to work for you on your next job.
- Assign friends to the same crew when feasible.
- Plan material handling and housekeeping.
- Keep toolbox meetings short and specific.

Training for Safety

- Attend foremen safety training courses.
- Learn how to run effective toolbox meetings.

The Safety Professional

We have called this part of the book "The Safety Professional." The people in the construction industry who have such jobs have a very wide variety of titles—"safety director," "safety engineer," "project safety coordinator," "field safety representative"—to name a few.

Someone meeting one of these safety professionals for the first time and hearing "safety" in the title might think that this person was responsible for safety, but, as safety professionals know, the truth of their jobs is more complicated. They are in staff rather than line positions; safety is a line responsibility. Therefore, the methods they use are directed toward the line managers who actually determine safety performance. Among their many activities:

- *They serve as consultants to management on the technical and organizational aspects of safety.*
- *They train managers so they can fulfill their safety responsibilities.*
- *They introduce record keeping and other systems to management by which supervisors can be held accountable for safety performance.*
- *They assist in the monitoring of safety performance for company projects.*
- *They help develop safety training and orientation materials.*
- *They introduce safety considerations into planning at all levels.*
- *They keep their organizations up to date on safety matters.*
- *Those with insurance responsibilities monitor insurance reserves and claims.*

▪ *In situations of imminent danger, they can shut down jobs.*

Excellent safety professionals recognize that improved project safety practices develop from the actions of job-site managers and foremen. They achieve safety objectives with line management by logical persuasion rather than through directives. Their influence is based on the societal need for safety that is reflected in the OSHA laws, their own expertise, their ability to work with others, and on the extent to which top management supports them.

We have divided the chapters in this section as follows:

Chapter 19. *We consider the safety professional's first task—getting straight in everyone's mind just who is responsible for safety performance. This means keeping out of what we call "the responsibility trap," i.e., the trap of being considered responsible for safety because of one's safety expertise—and one's designated title.*

Chapter 20. *We list methods which effective safety professionals use to gain the commitment of line managers to high safety performance.*

Chapter 21. *We describe the most effective safety performance measures for comparing companies and for supervisory accountability.*

Chapter 22. *We discuss a role safety professionals play beyond the confines of the company to which they belong: linking their company to outside safety-relevant groups.*

Chapter 23. *We consider the relationship between the size, type of construction, and location of work of construction firms and the size and role of their safety professional staff.*

Chapter 24. *We list a summary of action steps for safety professionals.*

In discussing these topics, we will draw on the experience of a number of safety professionals whom we have come to know well. They work in a variety of construction situations: for small, medium, and large construction companies as well as for insurance companies and insurance brokers. We also include in this section six illustrative cases of safety professionals who are either from construction companies with better-than-average safety records or from insurance organizations with a strong commitment to loss control for their client companies. (We will use fictitious names for these companies to maintain their privacy.)

Avoiding the
Responsibility Trap

The toughest part of the job of the safety professional is making sure that no one on any construction job thinks that safety professionals are responsible for safety. Unless managers at all levels are held accountable for safety performance and take that responsibility, safety professionals may feel good about their images in their companies as Mr. or Ms. Safety—until the resulting poor company safety record makes it clear that something is wrong.

The "responsibility trap" is easy to fall into, and it is defeating if one does. A staff safety person can be very tempted to take the credit for improvements in safety performance. But it is the operational units which have the safety records, not the safety professionals. It is the units who should get full credit. (The reverse situation may be easier for a staff safety person to see. Namely, that the job-site managers and the foremen are the ones who are falling down on the job when there is lack of safety improvement.)

What then is the role of the safety professionals if they are not responsible for safety? They provide expert guidance to top management, project management, foremen, and workers. They are monitors, advice givers, and support staff, but the job of putting decisions into operation is one for line management.

The safety professional, then, is there to help line managers fulfill their responsibilities. To be really successful, the safety person has to help line managers become as aware of safety violations and unsafe actions as the safety professional is. The most important task then is to teach others. Persuasion rather than formal authority is the key ingredient.

The safety professional depends upon several sources of informal authority: expertise, the societal belief in the importance of safety in the workplace as reflected in the OSHA laws, and top management support.

Importance of Top Management Support

The safety professionals we know are unanimous in emphasizing the value of support for safety from top management. When we asked the director of safety and insurance for Yeats, a construction company in highway and heavy construction, "What is the most important principle in doing a good job in your work on safety?", he answered:

> By far the most important thing is not just top management support, but top management involvement. Top management has to be a part of the accountability process and be involved in the identification of major safety problems and safety solutions. If there is accountability for safety on a routine basis, as a regular part of running the business, then the project managers will take the time to be involved.

This director of safety and insurance feels that top management can be involved either through "the importance of dollars saved or through the humanitarian aspect." He feels that the humanitarian works for him: "I tell my president: 'If we don't get these programs in place, we can kill someone.'" Other safety professionals find that presenting the facts on the money saved through safety is their most successful approach.

The importance of top management support and involvement can not be overestimated. Safety people mention it again and again when asked what helps them most in their work.

A safety engineer for Cole and Duncan, an industrial and commercial building construction company with an outstanding safety record, answers the question on the most important principle by saying: "The leadership at the top. They say: 'This is what we want. This is what we expect.'"

The director of safety and insurance for Hart & Johnson, a construction company which began with residential construction but now does nearly all their work in high-rise office buildings, hotels, hospitals, and airports answers: "Top management requires total high performance of their project managers and superintendents and will let them go if they do not perform well in safety or in any other important area."

A very experienced safety professional with Peters, a large insurance brokerage firm says: "I usually start right at the top with the top line and financial management people, demonstrating to them the financial costs of accidents. Once I have convinced them, my job is easy."

Keeping the Safety Perspective

Companies with outstanding safety records have methods for keeping the responsibility for safety where it belongs, with the project management people, and at the same time providing a means for making safety information and expertise a part of project operations.

The director of the safety department of Norton, a very large construction company with over a billion dollars yearly volume in heavy industrial construction—refineries, power plants, mass transit systems—states the following principles for their work:

1. Safety should be managed in the same way as productivity and quality.
2. The safety department is a service organization designed to provide professional service to their clients—the managers in the field.
3. In the field the safety representatives become integral members of the project teams and are responsible to the project manager on the project to which they are assigned.

When we turn to much smaller construction companies that have excellent safety records, we find the same strong belief that safety is a line management responsibility just as productivity is and the same view of safety professionals as service people to project management.

Harris, a company with a yearly volume of $300 million in high-rise building, makes the job superintendents responsible for safety on their projects. Their one full-time safety professional is considered the safety assistant to all the project superintendents.

Other companies with outstanding records designate project personnel to help with the safety function to supplement their safety professionals.

On each Cole & Duncan job, a company with an excellent safety record that has two full-time safety engineers, the job superintendent appoints a job safety representative. How much time the representative spends on safety compared to other duties depends on the size of the job, the number of subcontractors, and other factors. At peak periods on large jobs, the safety representatives might spend 100 percent of their time on safety, but more typically they spend about 10 percent. They usually check their jobs over a couple of times during the day and take care of any problems which they notice, such as putting up handrails which are missing or tieing in scaffolds. All of the Cole & Duncan foremen, however, are expected to do such things, so these are usually done automatically by whatever foreman on the job notices it first. The designated safety people are expected to be particularly aware of the subcontractors who may leave a potential hazard behind when they have finished working.

Hart and Johnson has a similar emphasis on giving project personnel safety responsibilities:

One of the job superintendents is designated the "job safety coordinator" on each of the company jobs. In addition every foreman is designated a safety inspector as are two union stewards: a carpenter steward and a laborer steward. The job safety coordinator, the foremen, and the two union stewards inspect the job each day.

Each of these companies has developed a successful method for maintaining both a special safety perspective on their projects and supervisory accountability for project safety.

Expertise and Skills in Human Relations

Safety professionals are in an advisory position to line management. They are, therefore, not able to order improvements in safety, except in situations of imminent danger. Yet each excellent safety professional has developed successful methods for demonstrating the value of safety.

Safety professionals generally find their interpersonal skills very helpful. Being able to talk easily with people at all levels in the company—from the CEO to the newest apprentice—is certainly an important part of the job. Being accepted as an expert to whom project personnel want to turn for help requires an ability to treat others as equals without losing sight of one's special knowledge, training, and skills.

This "special knowledge" aspect of the job can be called professionalism: having relevant safety information and knowledge at one's fingertips. Respect from all those with whom the safety professional comes into contact results from up-to-date knowledge not only of the area of safety and health but of construction. In Chapter 22 we will discuss further the many avenues by which safety professionals can continue to increase their knowledge and skills.

We shall describe next some of the methods excellent safety professionals use in working with line managers.

20

Buttressing Line Commitment

Once line managers have recognized that they are accountable for safety performance, is there a job left for the safety professional?

Yes, the real tasks of the safety professionals then become clear. They are the safety staff support for line management. Here we examine what they do to help the job-site managers and foremen maintain high safety performance on the job.

New-Worker Orientation Materials

Orienting new workers is a keystone to safety performance. In each of the different research studies—on top and job-site management and on foremen—those managers who did more new-worker orientation had the safer records. Safety professionals are the ones who communicate this truth about new workers to construction companies; they also develop orientation materials for each group.

The Yeats Engineering and Construction Company has highway and heavy construction projects in three states. Currently they have a craft workforce of 650 on 8 projects, 3 of them very large. Their new projects are often geographically distant from previous ones. On each project a large proportion of the craft workers are new hires from local areas in which there is little previous consciousness of or attention to safety.

To introduce such new hires to the project the safety director developed an orientation slide show in cooperation with top management and project management.

The basic orientation slide show is totally tailored to each job with slides showing the particular project, its special hazards, and how to deal with them. Viewing this slide show is required of every employee coming on the project.

Such a slide-tape or video presentation provides new employees with an overview of the company and project requirements and the project setting as well as demonstrating how to deal with special hazards. Having an orientation slide show which is totally tailored to each job may be more important for a company such as Yeats where each project is unique; for a company which specializes in one type of construction in one limited area, such as Cole & Duncan, a basic company orientation slide-tape show may be enough—perhaps with a few slides added for each unique site.

Cole & Duncan's orientation slide show was developed to be shown to each new employee. It features both Mr. Cole and Mr. Duncan, with Mr. Duncan making clear that safe job performance is a requirement at Cole & Duncan. The orientation slide show has reduced new-worker accidents substantially, fulfilling its planned purpose; it also has been useful in unexpected ways. The Cole & Duncan superintendents and foremen wanted to see it, so it was shown to them too. They enjoyed recognizing themselves and each other, but more importantly it affirmed the company's basic principles for them. Potential clients have also been impressed with it, making it an effective sales tool as well.

Slide shows are only one of many types of orientation materials which safety professionals develop. Booklets for new employees—emphasizing management's concern about safety and describing company and project work rules—are another type of useful orientation material. Close cooperation with job-site managers and foremen in the development of these materials ensures that they are an effective supplement to direct on-the-job orientation.

Training

Training is at the heart of the job of the safety professional. The task is to transfer safety expertise to line managers. Much of this teaching can be done informally, but a number of companies have found that formal training—accompanied by materials to take back to the job—is also necessary. Substantial investments of time and money are especially worthwhile when a construction company is working in locations far from their previous jobs with workers who are mostly new to the company.

The safety director at Yeats, for example, considered that the orientation slide show was not enough and is presently developing a loss-control manual for the company job-site managers and safety engineers. Each section of the manual will also become the course material for training in one aspect of safety and loss control.

The training program involves both formal classroom instruction and meetings on the job. Every 6 weeks the job-site managers, superintendents, and foremen on each project have a 3-hour classroom-type safety seminar on a special safety topic relevant to their work, such as crane safety or trenching and shoring. For these seminars the safety director hires specialists who are flown to the project area. He videotapes the specialist's presentation so that it will be available for others in the company later.

Another part of the formal classroom-type training is a management safety training course which takes place twice a year. Training is also built into the weekly supervisors meetings that are run by the safety engineers on the company's three big jobs and the weekly toolbox meetings that are run by the foremen for their crews. When the safety director goes on jobs, he often takes pictures of hazards and safety problems, which are then used in the training seminars and weekly meetings.

We talked earlier about the advantages to a company of being able to maintain a continuity of workers from job to job. Yeats, with their wide geographical spread, is not able to move a large proportion of their supervisors and workers from job to job. They, therefore, have invested more heavily in training than would be necessary for a company such as Cole & Duncan which works consistently in one part of one state and is able to move superintendents and foremen from a job that is finished to a new job that is starting up. Geographical spread, however, is not the only factor which increases the need for training. The same problem of supervisors and workers without previous experience with the company can arise if a company increases its volume rapidly so that its need for supervisors as well as workers outruns its available pool of people who have substantial experience on company projects.

The Hart and Johnson Construction Company has been growing rapidly in the last few years. Although all of their work is conducted in one state, they have had to expand their group of superintendents and foremen.

The safety and insurance director of Hart and Johnson conducts a 12-hour safety training course that is required for all its 161 project managers, superintendents, foremen, and field office managers. The course material is drawn from the safety director's 37 years of experience in construction safety and includes a wide variety of slides of construction safety violations which he has taken on jobs. The course also includes relevant safety films.

In addition, he also conducts a special 12-hour one-on-one safety training course for foremen who cannot read or write English.

15 Ways to Work Smarter in Underground

- Find out where utility mains (water, gas, electricity) involved with your work are and where the emergency shut offs are. Make sure all utilities are field located before you begin work.
- Test all confined spaces for toxic and deadly gases, flammable vapors, and oxygen deficiency *before each entry.*
- Make sure that trenches are properly sloped or shored and that there is someone readily available who can get help; even trenches in "solid rock" have caved in.
- Be aware that vibrations from equipment or nearby traffic can "liquefy" soil and cause cave-ins.
- Make certain that pipe is properly stored and handled; rolling pipe kills.
- Know what to do and who to contact in case of emergency; keep emergency telephone numbers where you can find them.
- Be alert when working near heavy equipment; the operator might not see you.

→

- Wear your personal protective equipment.
- Make sure that saws and other equipment have their proper guards in place.
- Keep electrical cords in good condition and out of the water.
- Make personally sure that the power is off before cutting any electrical line.
- Anticipate equipment contacting overhead power lines.
- Make personally sure that gas mains have been shut off, or located and adequately protected, before working near them.
- Be sure that your trench has the proper emergency exits at the proper spacings.
- Think. No one knows the hazards of your job better than YOU.

Developed by Stanford University Civil Engineering Construction Safety and Health Project, Stanford, CA 94305   **(415) 497-4447**

This material was prepared under grant number EJFOD342 from the Occupational Safety and Health Administration, U.S. Department of Labor. Points of view or opinions stated in this document do not necessarily reflect the views or policies of the U.S. Department of Labor.

FW0880

Figure 20.1   Pocket card to remind underground workers of safe behavior.

Safety professionals also develop materials to back up training such as the reminder cards for workers shown in Figures 20.1, 20.2, and 20.3.

New training programs and materials are developed to fill needs as they arise. Two recent areas are: (1) the identification and handling of employees with drug and alcohol problems and (2) storage and handling of hazardous substances on job sites.

Toolbox Meetings

Foremen and other line managers usually run the weekly toolbox meetings, but there are a number of ways which safety professionals have developed to make these meetings more effective:

- Weekly safety newsletters, written and/or edited by safety staff members, which feature relevant topics for foremen to use if they do not have a topic arising directly from their work.
- Organizing a planning group of foremen to develop a series of suggested topics which can then be distributed.
- Organizing training sessions for foremen to help them develop skills in conducting toolbox meetings.
- Developing checklists or reminder sheets for conducting toolbox meetings.

Job Visits

Most construction projects have no on-site safety professionals. Instead, staff from the home office make frequent job-site visits. These job visits are the most usual way in which safety professionals—whether from insurance companies or the company itself—relate to project personnel. While the main purpose of these visits is to monitor the job for safety performance, they also provide opportunities for training and for obtaining feedback on job problems.

At Cole & Duncan Construction Company the safety engineers's time in the field is spent primarily on job visits—walking the job and talking with the craft workers and foremen. When the safety engineer walks through the workplace, he also looks at places where work has been done or may be starting soon. This time in the field involves many activities other than safety inspections. For example, it may include informal on-the-job training with an individual or a few workers where appropriate or discussions with foremen and workers on OSHA regulations or on ways to do particular tasks safely. The most important function, according to the safety engineer, is to keep the safety message before the workforce.

Figure 20.2 Pocket cards developed for roofers.

TYPE OF WELDING	HAZARD	SOURCE	MATERIAL	EFFECT	CONTROL
Arc acetylene	fumes	metal being welded; electrode used; coating on metal; flux; filler metals	cadmium, cobalt, lead, antimony, chromium, copper, iron, beryllium, magnesium, manganese, tin, zinc, fluorides	metal fume fever, irritates lungs; dry throat and cough, nausea, headache, chills with fever, aching in joints, loss of appetite	local exhaust ventilation; respirator if in confined area
Arc especially inert gas weld	non-ionizing radiation	welding arc	infrared and ultraviolet	irritates and damages eye tissue; can cause painful sunburn and possibly skin cancer	tinted glass to shield welder; proper eye protection and body covering including all exposed skin; separate welders from other workers; welding screens
Arc acetylene	toxic gases	the arc, burning process or changes in the atmosphere	acetylene, arsine, carbon dioxide, carbonic acid, carbon monoxide, nitrogen dioxide, ozone, phosgene, phosphine	some symptoms—headache; nausea; irritates lungs; eyes, nose and skin; dizziness and lack of appetite	respirator if in confined area; good local exhaust ventilation
Arc acetylene	metallic sparks, molten metal	sparks from heated metal; hot metal	all metals	burns, fires	eye protection; clothing—pants, long sleeves and socks; gloves
Arc	high voltage	splices, wires		shocks, fires	keep electrodes covered, keep all electric cable splices and wires in good condition, avoid welding in damp area
Arc	solvent vapors	cleaning and degreasing of metals before welding; ultraviolet rays in welding decompose degreasing solvents	trichloroethylene and other chlorinated hydrocarbons; degreasing solvents can produce deadly phosgene gas on exposure to ultraviolet rays of arc	can be fatal; irritates skin, eyes, nose, throat and chest; dizziness; chills; thirst; delayed effect: fluid in lungs and death.	no welding within 200 ft. of degreasing operations; if gas smelled, welding should be stopped immediately and area evacuated

See a physician if overexposure to welding fumes is suspected.

Figure 20.3 Sample page from booklet developed for welders.

What the safety professional does while visiting jobs may be quite diverse. One excellent safety engineer, for example, states that a great deal of his time is spent in saying hello and shaking hands with people all over each of the jobs he visits. He considers this time well spent; without that personal contact, he would not hear about problems before they develop into accidents. The importance of being available is stressed again and again by highly experienced safety professionals. As the safety director of Hart and Johnson says:

It is very important to be visible to the project people. They can handle safety problems 99.9 percent of the time themselves, but they need to be able to turn to me when they can't solve the problems themselves.

The safety professional for Harris Company, which specializes in high-rise buildings, spends almost three-quarters of her time in the field. She considers that these job visits help the superintendents maintain safety awareness among all the workers. She stresses:

> Keep them thinking about safety on the job so that they don't begin to work routinely and automatically. To keep a safe workplace, you have to stay aware of the safety aspects of the task. When the work gets automatic, that's when accidents happen because people are not thinking about what they are doing.

Although safety professionals accomplish many different tasks during job visits, top managements often rate inspections their most important one. At Cole & Duncan for example:

> Top management considers the field safety engineer's main job to be inspecting jobs and documenting these inspections. One of the most important parts of this is to monitor the activities of the subcontractors. If the craftsmen in the subcontractor's workforce are not protecting themselves adequately, the safety engineer seeks out their foreman and discusses it with him. If a problem is still not resolved, it is brought up in a meeting between the project superintendent and the subcontractor's management.

The Harris safety professional reports that she is evaluated "by the vice president of Field Operations who walks jobs himself and monitors such things as housekeeping and how the subcontractors are operating."

Another method by which safety professionals help line management improve safety performance is in the selection of effective safety performance measures. These measures for monitoring line management at all levels are discussed in the next chapter.

21

Measuring Safety Performance

One of the most important jobs for safety professionals is that of advising management on safety performance measures. Contractors use these measures to monitor their own companies, to select and monitor their subcontractors, to maintain line accountability for safety, and to pinpoint problem areas. Buyers use them to select and to monitor contractors.

Safety performance measures are used primarily to compare different units or groups of individuals and also to compare one unit or group of individuals over time. In this chapter we shall consider two general levels of comparisons: companies and supervisors. We will review alternative methods for measuring safety performance and discuss their relative effectiveness, and we will then discuss the use of safety measures to highlight problem areas.

Company Safety Performance

Company-level safety performance measures have a number of uses. Top managers of construction companies use them to gauge their firm's progress and to compare their safety record to their competition, buyers use them to select general contractors, and general contractors use them to select subcontractors.

There are a two different types of measures presently in use which fulfill these functions effectively under certain conditions: experience modification ratings (EMR) and OSHA reportable injury incidence rates.

Experience modification ratings

In Chapter 1 we discussed the relationship of the EMR to the size of insurance premium which an employer pays for workers' compensation. We explained in that section that in calculating EMRs the rating bureaus take into account each company's insurance claims costs compared to other companies with similar risks. Therefore, EMRs provide a useful method for comparing a company's safety performance with that of other similar companies. However, as with any measure, one needs to know its limits:

- EMRs are not reflective of the present safety performance of a company since the latest EMR is based on an average of the company's performance 4, 3, and 2 years ago.
- Very small companies may not be eligible for experience rating and, even when they are, their EMRs will be not be as good a reflection of their own claims experience as they are for larger companies. For example, California employers with less than $13,100 in premiums (based on manual rates) were no longer eligible for experience rating after January 1, 1986.
- New companies or new joint ventures are automatically rated at 100.
- The reserving practices of the contractor's insurance company and a contractor's practices on monitoring of reserves can affect EMRs.

Taking these limitations into account, EMRs are nevertheless effective safety performance measures for comparisons among companies. Contractors can use them to compare their own firm's performance with competitors. Buyers find them helpful in selecting contractors and contractors use them to select among key subcontractors.

OSHA recordable incidence rate

Another safety performance measure which is generally available for comparisons between companies is the OSHA recordable incidence rate. This rate is based on a company's entries from the Log and Summary of the OSHA no. 200 form. The yearly total for fatalities, injuries, and illnesses with lost workdays and injuries and illnesses without lost workdays are used. The other information needed to calculate the incidence rate comes from payroll or other time records: the number of hours all employees actually worked during the year (hours worked should not include any nonwork time, even though paid such as vacation, sick leave, holidays, etc.). The formula used by the Bureau of Labor Statistics, Department of Labor is:

$$\text{Incidence rate} = \frac{\text{number of injuries and illnesses} \times 200,000}{\text{employee hours worked}}$$

(The 200,000 hours in the formula represent the equivalent of 100 employees working 40 hours per week, 50 weeks per year, and it provides the standard base for the incidence rates.)

The Bureau of Labor Statistics of the U.S. Department of Labor computes yearly occupational injury and illness incidence rates by industry. Until recently you could send for a booklet developed for the construction industries called *Evaluating Your Firm's Injury and Illness Record,* but at the time this book was written the booklet was no longer being published. Contractors wanting to compare their safety records with others doing similar types of construction should calculate their incidence rates using the formula described above. They then should call the nearest Bureau of Labor Statistics Regional Office to obtain the average incidence rate for their type of construction. The statistics are organized into the following categories of construction:

1. Under general building contractors
   a. Nonresidential building construction
   b. Operative builders
   c. Residential building construction

2. Under heavy construction contractors
   a. Heavy construction, except highway
   b. Highway and street construction

3. Under special trade contractors
   a. Carpentering and flooring
   b. Concrete work
   c. Electrical work
   d. Masonry, stonework, and plastering
   e. Miscellaneous special trade contractors
   f. Painting, paper hanging, and decorating
   g. Plumbing, heating, and air conditioning
   h. Roofing and sheet-metal work
   i. Water well drilling

This method of evaluating company safety performance permits the company incidence rate to be compared to the average incidence rate for all companies in that type of construction. These statistics are available from the Bureau of Labor Statistics typically in April of the second year after the one from which the data is compiled. This means that there is a lag of at least a year and one-quarter before contractors can compare their accident records of a given year with those of comparable contractors for that year. In Table 21.1 we list the figures issued by the Bureau of Labor Statistics for the years 1983 and 1984.

Compared to the EMR, the OSHA recordable incidence rate has the

TABLE 21.1   Occupational Injury and Illness Incidence Rates

	Average incidence rates per 100 full-time workers	
Type of construction	1983	1984
General building contractors	14.4	15.4
Nonresidential building	17.3	18.9
Residential building	11.9	12.6
Operative builders	9.7	11.5
Heavy construction contractors	15.4	14.9
Heavy construction, except highway	15.9	15.1
Highway and street construction	14.3	14.6
Special trade contractors	14.8	15.8
Plumbing, heating, air conditioning	15.7	16.4
Painting, paperhanging, decorating	9.2	10.3
Electrical work	13.7	14.4
Masonry, stonework, plastering	15.8	17.3
Carpentry and flooring	13.1	14.9
Roofing and sheet-metal work	18.6	21.4
Concrete work	14.2	14.6
Water well drilling	11.3	12.9
Miscellaneous special trades	15.1	15.8

SOURCE: Bureau of Labor Statistics, Table 1, Occupational injury and illness rates by industry, 1983 and 1984.

advantage of being more recent and of being applicable to small companies as well as to medium-sized and large ones. Its disadvantage is that it is less objective because companies may not use exactly the same definitions of what is an OSHA recordable case. When used together with the latest average incidence rates from the Bureau of Labor Statistics, it is a valuable supplement to the EMR both for comparisons by contractors of their firms' safety records with other comparable firms and for the selection of contractors and subcontractors.

Gauging company improvement

Both a company's EMR and its OSHA reportable incidence rate are useful in evaluating its safety performance over a number of years. The EMR is a 3-year average which reflects a company's comparative position in relation to other companies doing similar work. The main disadvantage of EMRs as measures of company performance over time is the fact that last year's record is not included. A company's OSHA reportable incidence rate over a number of years is therefore a useful supplement to the company's EMR trend as it can include last year's performance.

Supervisory Accountability

Safety professionals affect job-site management by their recommended methods for monitoring safety performance. With these accident measures, they compile statistics for senior and project management which can then be used to create accountability for safety.

Accidents and their costs need to be monitored for each job in order to ensure that project management—project managers, superintendents, and foremen—take safety management seriously and maintain it as a high priority. But monitoring project accidents and their costs is not enough. Accountability for safety depends upon an effective record-keeping system with figures which make sense to both project management and top management. Otherwise top management may exert counterproductive pressures on project management.

In Chapter 3, "Putting Accident Costs Up Front," we recommended that construction companies monitor safety performance with an accident cost system since such a system relies on costs, the common denominator for many other aspects of job performance. Safety professionals with the responsibility for helping a company choose the measure of safety performance for a line management accountability and reward system will want to review Part 1 (with special emphasis on Chapter 3) for details. Here we summarize the most relevant parts of that discussion.

Using accident costs

One effective method for gauging supervisory safety performance uses the Stanford Accident Cost Schedule. The process involves finding the appropriate costs on the cost schedule and then "charging" the cost of each accident to those supervisors who have responsibility for supervising the worker who had the accident. Thus the cost of one accident would be charged to the worker's foreman, that foreman's general foreman, the appropiate superintendent, and the job-site manager. In order to make fair comparisons between different foremen, general foremen, and job-site managers, the accident cost totals for each supervisor are then divided by the total employee hours worked by those supervised. This provides an effective safety performance measure for supervisory accountability: accident costs per employee hour worked.

A number of companies calculate this cost measure on a monthly basis for all of their supervisors including foremen. These reports are organized to make comparisons among supervisors easy and are sent to upper management and supervisors.

If a firm is engaged in widely different types of construction—e.g., residential building construction and dam construction—accident cost data should be normalized before the safety performance of the supervisors on these different projects are directly compared.

The average manual or "book" rate of workers' compensation insurance premiums on each project, *expressed in dollars per work hour*, represents the mix of workers' compensation insurance premium categories used on each project. It, therefore, takes the variation in risk between the different types of construction work into account. If this measure is used to adjust the *accident cost per workhour* for supervisors on different projects, supervisors' safety performance can be directly compared across widely different types of construction.

Since the Accident Cost Accounting Schedule provides *predicted* costs rather than actual costs, some companies prefer to substitute the actual claims costs for the predicted costs when they become available from their insurance companies. In either case it is important to divide by the number of employee hours supervised to obtain a comparable measure of safety performance for supervisors with different sizes of work groups.

Using OSHA reportables

The total number of OSHA reportable accidents for a project during a given period includes fatalities, injuries, and illnesses with and without lost workdays. This measure is a better reflection of project safety performance than just injuries and illnesses *with* lost workdays. Since a broader range of accidents is included, such a system is less likely to make poor safety performers at the job-site manager level seem like good ones. To make comparisons between different projects, however, it is fairer to use a measure which takes into account the number of hours worked on the project, as the larger the number of employee hours worked, the greater the exposure to injuries. The OSHA reportables injury incidence formula described in the previous section of this chapter is therefore useful for comparing supervisors as well as companies.

The primary disadvantage of using the OSHA reportable incidence to compare supervisors is that it is not in the job language of costs. Since the main reason for comparing supervisors is to create accountability for safety performance, there are definite advantages to using a measure which describes safety performance in dollars and cents. Safety professionals who rely on the OSHA reportable incidence as their primary measure of project safety performance have the continuing task of convincing both top management and project supervision that these numbers are indirect reflections of costs. As we have pointed out in Part 1, accidents create real costs which should be tied to the supervisors who produce them. Supervisors, therefore, are likely to treat the OSHA reportable incidence less seriously than those elements of the job which are reported in dollars and cents.

Both accident costs per employee hour worked and the OSHA reportable incidence are valuable measures for evaluating supervisory safety performance.

Problems in using lost-time accidents

We have all driven up to a project that has a big sign out front proclaiming the number of days the project has gone without a lost-time accident. Here, the number of lost-time accidents is being used as the measure of construction safety performance. Although this method provides a common, easily understood goal for all project personnel, its disadvantages outweigh this one advantage.

(The careful reader will notice an apparent inconsistency on this topic; we ourselves in other chapters have used lost-time accidents to describe the safety records of outstanding project managers and foremen. We were forced to use it; it was the only measure by which these and other supervisors were measured over many years. We are looking forward to the time when this is no longer true.)

Using the number of lost-time accidents as a measure of either company or project safety performance has three serious disadvantages: (1) the relative infrequency of lost-time accidents, (2) the encouragement it gives to keeping "the walking wounded" on the job, and (3) the fact that lost-time accidents by themselves are a poor reflection of insurance costs.

Lost-time accidents are relatively rare events. Their statistical infrequency means that they are difficult to use in creating month-to-month accountability for project managers and are useless at the foremen level. Thus, using this measure alone can make project managers and foremen look as though they are doing a good job when in fact they may not be.

The second problem with using lost-time accidents alone is that it encourages project managers to keep their injured on the job. The message which is sent by such a record-keeping approach is that non-lost-time accidents and first aid accidents are expected as part of construction, while job-site managers are accountable for their lost-time accidents and are expected to control them. One easy way for job-site managers to "control" lost-time accidents is to make very clear to all project personnel that injured people should come right back on the job after an accident if they can possibly do so—even if they cannot be productive and may even hinder the effectiveness of others. (Such a practice can make for strange accidents; we discovered one going over a company's records; a carpenter with a broken arm re-injured it by using the cast as a hammer!)

We are saying here that the practice of returning workers as soon as possible to the job should not be undertaken to artificially give an excellent safety record to a project manager who in reality has had a number of accidents occur on the job. There may, however, be other very good reasons for encouraging workers to return to the job, such as improving their morale and hastening their recovery.

The use of lost-time accidents by themselves as a measure of safety performance is especially deceptive as a means of reflecting accident costs. On one dam-building project that was reported in the foreman study (Samelson, 1977), there was only one lost-time accident during the project's 11 months, but during the same period there were 142 accident cases requiring medical aid, 669 first aid cases, and one death. The bills for medical claims therefore were much more substantial than the one lost-time accident would ever lead one to suspect. Even more important for insurance premium costs, the company's experience modification rating would reflect the medical aid cases since frequency is weighed more heavily than severity in the EMR formula (see Chapter 1 for details). Furthermore, as we reported in Chapter 2, the hidden cost multiplier is greater for non-lost-time accidents. Yet if the widespread reliance on lost-time accidents as the primary indicator of safety performance had been in effect for that company, the job-site manager on that job might well have earned a safety award, despite the very substantial costs incurred for accidents. Such award-winning job-site managers can increase a company's EMR rather than decrease it. Accident costs are very poorly reflected by measuring only lost-time accidents. Safety professionals should, therefore, try to encourage their managers to use more effective safety performance measures.

Using Measures for Finding Problem Areas

Another important use of accident statistics is to discover areas which need special attention. This type of use requires that injury data be recorded so that it can be categorized in various ways.

Categorizing injuries by the part of the body affected.   This allows the safety professional to monitor body part injury frequency. A high percentage, or a sudden increase, of eye injuries, for example, might suggest reviewing the use of safety glasses and goggles.

Categorizing injuries by type of injury.   This can indicate if there are large number of workers with certain special injury types. For example, if many accidents were strains, the safety professional might look into project procedures for lifting and handling materials.

Categorizing injuries by length of time worker has been on the job.   This is necessary to monitor the success of new-worker orientation.

Categorizing injuries by craft of injured worker.   This may bring out that one craft is having a particular type of problem which can then be corrected.

There are many other useful categories such as age of injured worker, sex of injured worker, and source of injury (hand tools, vehicles, etc.). Safety professionals need to consider which categories will be most useful to them so that these can be included in the necessary forms for recording accidents. These should then be tested for their value as indicators of problem areas and revisions should then be made if necessary.

Future Measures

All of the preceding measures are based on accidents and injuries. As construction safety management becomes more and more successful, that very success will require the development of positive indicators of safety management. Safety professionals have long dreamed of developing ways to measure safe behavior in the workplace rather than measuring the outcomes of unsafe behavior. There are two types of positive measures which need development.

One type is the measurement of safety management methods themselves. Thus an inventory could be developed for each level of management using the material presented in this book. It would include ratings of a particular manager on the appropriate safety management methods. For example, job-site managers would be rated on their new-worker orientation programs, their training of foremen for orientation, their communication networks, their long-range people building skills, their planning, etc. The prediction would be that the manager who is successfully doing these actions will have high safety performance, but there is still a need for another type of measure, a measure of outcome, of whether, in fact, these management methods did lead to safe worker performance.

This other type is the measurement of safe work behaviors. At present the only method for developing such measures would seem to be the careful observation of specific jobs, a very long and painstaking task. The development of such indicators of worker safety performance is a task for the future.

Summary

This review of safety performance measures considers two main uses for them: comparisons among companies and comparisons among supervisors. In addition, safety performance measures are also used as a means for pinpointing problem areas.

Experience modification ratings and OSHA reportable injury incidence rates are recommended for comparing safety performance at the
company level.

Safety professionals may well find that the function of monitoring
supervisors can best be served by the direct and well-understood
measure of accident costs, for example, some form of accident cost
accounting. As we have pointed out in earlier chapters, line accountability for safety is emphasized when managers are made responsible
for directly stated accident costs as well as other job costs. Details on
an accident cost accounting system are given in Chapter 3.

Reexamining the often-used method of counting only lost-time
accidents (and ignoring non-lost-time and first aid cases) demonstrates
that its disadvantages outweigh its advantages as a means for creating
supervisory accountability for safety performance.

Safety professionals also use performance measures to point to areas
needing improvement. This use requires that accident data be categorized. Useful categories include part of body affected, type of injury,
length of time on the job, and craft of worker.

Present safety performance measures are outcome measures, i.e.,
they are based on the occurrence of injuries and their costs. As
construction safety management becomes more successful, the need
will grow for process, or behavioral, measures of safety performance.
Two types of process measures suggested for study are those gauging
the safety management methods of managers and those gauging the
safe behaviors of workers.

Chapter
22

Working with
Outside Groups

Safety professionals in construction companies are usually the company's safety representative to other groups. While these contacts usually represent a small fraction of time, they are very important.

There are, of course, the national associations. The American Society of Safety Engineers has local groups with many programs of general interest to all those working in the area of safety and health. Furthermore in a number of geographical areas there is also a special construction division in which safety engineers working with construction companies can swap know-how and hear relevant speakers. Both the construction division of the American Society of Safety Engineers and the National Safety Council's construction safety section provide special programs at their annual conferences.

The general construction associations such as the National Constructors Association (NCA), the Associated General Contractors (AGC), and the Associated Builders and Contractors (ABC) and the associations of the various specialty contractors (such as the Electrical Contractors Association) are another valuable set of outside groups. These organizations all have national committees that are concerned with safety and health and often have state and regional groups as well. Construction safety company representatives not only have the opportunity through these associations to attend meetings at which new information is presented, but they can also join with others to develop common materials and plan concerted actions.

Another set of valuable groups for construction safety professionals are the national and state occupational safety and health administration staffs. The professionals in the consultation section of the state

OSHA group are especially useful to contact during the planning of a job. Such contact allows their input to be utilized at an early enough stage of the process so that job management can set up procedures and methods to lower injuries and decrease the potential for fines as well. Both on-the-job and formal training are also available from the state and national OSHA organizations, as are a number of booklets and other materials which can be useful in training managers and workers.

For safety professionals working with unionized construction companies, the building trade unions are another very important group to contact and work with. A number of unions, for example, the Operating Engineers, have their own job safety representatives. Both the Building and Construction Trades Department of the American Federation of Labor and the national and international organizations of the different building trade unions also have their own staffs of safety and health professionals who can work with company safety representatives. Joint activities range from informal activities such as walk-arounds of jobs to such major cooperative programs as the voluntary self-inspection projects which involve agreements between construction companies, unions, and OSHA.

Colleges and universities with construction courses and safety management courses can be another source of valuable information. In addition they often have the knowledge and skills to set up special fact-finding studies.

All of these groups provide opportunities for construction safety professionals to broaden their understanding and increase their ability to support and strengthen the safety goals of their line management. They also make possible the development of cooperative materials and programs so that each individual company safety department or safety representative does not have to reinvent the wheel.

23

Finding the Best Fit

How should companies decide whether or not they should have one or more full-time safety professionals on their staff? How many should they have? What should the safety professionals be doing? In this chapter we will present some illustrative answers to these questions.

Our aim is to show how the jobs of safety professionals vary to fit the particular needs of a company. In order to illustrate varied roles for safety staff in different construction situations, we shall look at six case studies of safety professionals: one in an insurance brokerage that has a strong commitment to loss control for their client companies and five who are working in construction companies.

Staff from Insurance Brokers and Carriers

What are the pros and cons of relying solely on safety professionals from insurance companies and brokerages? Many small construction companies currently have no safety professionals on their staffs. Instead they use the safety personnel of their insurance carrier and/or broker, sharing services with a number of other clients. To find out what construction companies can expect from this arrangement we will examine the services available from an insurance broker. (As noted earlier, fictional names are used for the companies in order to preserve their privacy.)

The Peters Company is a large nationwide insurance brokerage firm with a staff of approximately 8000 in the United States; of these about 150 have full-time responsibilities for safety. These safety specialists work with their clients, the buyers of insurance, and also coordinate with the insurance carrier's loss-control consultants.

In general the carrier's loss-control consultants spend the majority of their field time walking jobs and talking with project people about inspection results and writing reports on their inspections for the insurance company's underwriters.

The Peters Company safety personnel work with the clients to design safety management programs for them and to audit these programs. Their main approach is motivational and financial. They work with each client's designated safety officer and with each client's financial people.

The top management of the Peters Company considers that the safety professionals' main job is to keep their clients happy. This means producing long-range results which will reduce their clients' experience modification ratings (EMR) and increase their dividends. Top management of the Peters Company uses EMR trends, injury frequency, and feedback from their clients to decide whether the safety people are doing a good job.

The safety staff operates out of regional offices with each major office doing its own staffing. In addition to serving their clients, there is interchange between the various offices so that the nearest office will service a particular project or plant in a particular region even if another office has the insurance account.

The role that the brokerage safety professional fills for a particular construction company depends upon the extent to which the construction company has a safety staff of its own. Among Peters' construction clients, relatively few have much staff. Their client construction companies frequently have someone who is designated as a safety officer or safety director who devotes some proportion of time to safety; often this person has not had any formal safety training. Some companies rely solely on Peters and/or the insurance carrier for help in safety.

Peters' safety-related activities can be divided into two types: (1) contacts with the client's top operations and financial managers and (2) contacts with the client's plant or field personnel. The time spent in the field is roughly divided as follows:

- 35 percent site inspections
- 15 percent keeping up to date on OSHA regulations and communicating to others about them
- 10 percent safety training
- 10 percent investigating accidents

In addition, time is spent attending safety meetings in client companies; attending professional meetings, reading journals, and obtaining additional formal training; providing information on new methods and equipment to clients; representing safety considerations in client planning; devising and running safety incentive programs; and doing a variety of other activities, including relating to carrier safety personnel.

The safety professionals working for insurance brokerage firms and insurance carriers have to spread themselves among a number of clients. A company depending upon them as their only safety professional staff cannot expect much assistance. The professionals are often experienced and capable, but their time is very limited—much less than a half-time safety professional for a company would provide.

Furthermore, their clients represent many types of companies with diverse safety and health problems. They may or may not have a number of other construction companies as clients; they may or may not have knowledge about the specialized area of construction safety. Certainly they cannot specialize in construction safety, as they have to serve their clients in their different businesses.

Whether construction companies are thinking of using safety professionals from insurance brokerages and carriers as their sole safety staff or to augment in-house staff, they need to evaluate the services they will receive. Before choosing an insurance carrier, companies with outstanding safety records find out what kind of statistical analysis they will obtain of accident costs and how often information will be provided and how detailed it will be; for example, will there be monthly reports which list medical costs by foremen and job-site managers? They also check the reserving policies of companies they are considering—an insurance company with a very conservative reserving policy can be very costly, as we discussed in Chapter 1. Evaluation of the potential safety staff services from either an insurance broker or carrier should cover the type of services offered to clients and the frequency of these services.

Staff in Construction Companies

The increased cost of accidents is making more construction companies seriously consider having their own safety staff; this trend is supported by research results which indicate that companies with in-house safety professionals have experience modification ratings 14 percent lower than those without them (Levitt, 1975).

Our illustrative cases will describe five construction companies which have a staff of one or more safety professionals. In these descriptions we will relate the number of safety professionals and their duties to the different types of work, geographical spread, and size and makeup of the workforce of the five companies.

The following summary gives an overview of these construction companies:

Name	$ Volume	No. of craft workers	No. of safety staff	Craft workers per staff	EMR
Cole & Duncan	200 million	450	2.5	180.0	48
Harris	300 million	235	1.0	235.0	71
Yeats	60 million	650	4.0	162.5	77
Hart and Johnson	250 million	500	1.0	500.0	89
Norton	over a billion	20,000	77.0	259.7	69

This summary of the five construction companies describes a few of their characteristics to form a background for the detailed descriptions of the jobs of safety professionals and their companies. The five companies show contrasts in dollar volume, number of craft workers, number of safety professionals, number of craft workers per safety professional, and, to some extent, EMR (48 to 89).

> As the chart shows, Cole & Duncan Construction Company has an enviable safety record. Even though they have been growing steadily in recent years, their safety record has continued to be outstanding: an EMR of only 48. Their specialty is industrial and commercial building construction, and their work is concentrated in one area of one state. They currently have 30 projects with the number of workers on a given project ranging from 3 to over 100.
>
> Two people in Cole & Duncan have safety as their full-time responsibility. In addition, the department supervisor to whom they report spends about one-half of his time on safety. One of the safety engineers spends three-quarters of his time in the field visiting projects, while the other divides his time equally between the field and administration. The number of craft workers per safety professional is the next to the lowest of the five: 180.

Since Cole & Duncan consistently has jobs in one section of one state, they can move workers and supervisors from job to job, reducing the number of new workers they have to train. Even with this lower-than-average turnover, they are strong on training—with their own new-worker orientation slide-tape show, a program of sending their foremen for safety training, and the in-house development of other training aids such as a slide-tape program on the use of protective equipment and a hazardous materials booklet. To supplement the field visits of their safety professionals, they use on-site safety representatives and also expect the foremen to inspect their sections of the job on a daily basis and correct any hazards they find. Their excellent safety record then is due to top management involvement and commitment combined with supervisory and worker training and accountability and good safety professional support in a working situation which makes high continuity of supervision and craft workers possible.

Like Cole & Duncan, Harris specializes in one type of construction, high-rise building, and concentrates even more heavily in a limited geographical area—working only in one city. Harris has a safety staff of one person who is responsible for both safety and insurance loss control.

The Harris safety professional spends 70 percent of her time visiting the 20 company jobs, making site inspections, and driving between them. The other 30 percent of her time is spent in nonfield activities: in necessary paper work and in contacts with OSHA personnel and lawyers, as the company's representative. While the record keeping for accidents is handled by the time keeper, she reviews all of these records.

Part of her office time is spent organizing the necessary materials for new jobs. Before each new job starts, she obtains the necessary OSHA permits for the job and collects such materials needed for the job as the material data sheets, the bulletin board posters, record-keeping forms, etc.

In addition to the safety component of her job, she also has loss-control responsibilities. In particular she represents the company in legal actions such as third-party lawsuits for which she writes interrogatories and meets with lawyers. She also handles their workers' compensation insurance and insurance claims for auto accidents and property liability cases.

Since Harris primarily concentrates on high-rise building in one city, they are able to maintain high supervisory continuity and considerable worker continuity as well. Their supervisors and workers know the company's requirements for safe, productive work; they have therefore less need for extensive training. One safety professional is workable both because of Harris's emphasis on superintendent responsibility for safety performance—with the safety professional as staff to each job-site manager—and because of the relatively high proportion of supervisors and workers who have worked for them previously.

In contrast to Harris and to Cole & Duncan with their high concentrations of jobs in one geographic locality and their specialization in one type of construction, the Yeats Engineering and Construction Company has eight highway and heavy construction projects spread over three states. As we mentioned in Chapter 20 in discussing new-worker orientation and training, Yeats' projects are usually in areas distant from their previous jobs, requiring many new hires. Yeats has a safety professional on each of their three large projects in addition to having a director of safety and insurance.

The director of safety and insurance for Yeats combines a broad background of experience in insurance loss control and risk management and has a degree in safety engineering as well as many years in construction. He divides his time as follows: 40 percent on the total safety function, 40 percent on risk management and insurance, 15 percent on management and administration, and 5 percent on travel.

As part of the safety function, he develops and evaluates the corporate safety policy and ensures that it is implemented on the job. He also reviews the safety records and plans the necessary safety training for all levels. Another part of this function is attending meetings with job-site management, with owners, and with the three safety engineers on the largest jobs.

His time spent on risk management and insurance involves him in workers' compensation insurance and many other types of insurance (approximately 28) which the company carries. In this aspect of his job he evaluates what the company's loss exposures are, how to deal with these exposures including evaluating appropriate insurance carriers and placing the company's insurance with the carriers. In areas such as major property or equipment, he spends considerable time documenting losses, presenting them to the carriers, and negotiating with them. Another aspect of this part of his job is working with lawyers.

Yeats has the lowest number of craft workers per safety professional of the five companies studied. This higher proportion of safety professionals to craft workers compensates for the size and diversity of their projects and their geographical separation as well as for their very high proportion of supervisors and workers new to the company. Their proportionally larger safety staff, their emphasis on orientation, training, and accountability, combined with strong top management support, makes Yeats able to maintain a better-than-average EMR despite potentially negative job factors.

The Hart and Johnson Construction Company, in contrast to Yeats, has the highest proportion of craft workers to safety professionals in our small group of cases.

The Hart and Johnson Construction Company began with residential construction, but now nearly all their work is high-rise office buildings, hotels, hospitals, and airports. Their yearly volume has been rising rapidly. They currently have 23 projects. The number of craft workers per project ranges from 150 on one project to none on two projects for which Hart and Johnson is the construction manager. All of their work is conducted in one state. Although their EMR is around average at 89, their reductions in lost-time and nonlost-time accidents in the last few years should reduce their next year's EMR.

The Hart and Johnson safety professional has the title of safety and insurance director. He is responsible for formulating, implementing, and monitoring safety inspection, training, and incentive programs for all employees and administering insurance, safety, and security procedures for all projects.

On a daily basis he makes safety and security inspections of jobs; provides advice on safety, insurance, and security matters; and administers workers' compensation and liability insurance programs including coordinating with the insurance broker and insurance carriers.

Other activities include writing a biweekly company safety newsletter, calculating monthly and quarterly safety bonuses, making monthly job inspections with CAL/OSHA and insurance carrier representatives, conducting a formal supervisory 12-hour construction safety training course once a year, and preparing defenses for attorneys on third-party liability suits and on CAL/OSHA citations and appeals.

When he first came on the job, he reviewed the practices and services offered by the company's main insurance carrier. Finding that they had been keeping very high reserves on unclosed claims, were slow to remove reserves after the injured worker had returned to work, did not offer a pertinent loss-control program to the company, and did not understand building construction safety, he recommended to the company that they change carriers—a recommendation top management accepted. As part of the insurance side of his job, he monitors the company's insurance carrier reserve practices and works with the insurance brokers and carriers who insure their different projects.

The location of Hart and Johnson's work—in one state, much of it within commuting distance—helps their safety professional keep on top of his many duties and responsibilities. Another helpful factor is his emphasis on supervisory accountability and training, thus reducing the dependence of supervisors on him. The ratio of 500 craft workers to 1 safety professional at Hart and Johnson requires heavy reliance on job-site managers to provide the day-by-day guidance on safety for their projects.

We have now sampled various roles which safety professionals play in all but the very large construction companies. Norton is a firm which employs 20,000 craft workers and does a yearly volume of over a billion dollars. Their full-time safety people have a variety of jobs.

In Norton there are 77 people who have safety as their main responsibility with 9 of them located in home or regional offices and 68 of them in the field on construction projects.

The older staff members have developed their expertise through many years of experience in construction and construction safety, while the younger ones typically have degrees in safety engineering, industrial hygiene, or related areas.

Although the field safety personnel are assigned by the home office safety group, they are responsible to the project manager on the project to which they are assigned.

The home office safety staff members spend most of their time working with management on safety issues and with field safety people on planning and personnel considerations.

The field safety people spend their time as follows:

- About 25 percent working with different levels of supervisors on planning safety into the work operations.
- About 25 percent working with supervisors on solving specific project questions as they arise such as developing a plan for handling a particular hazardous substance or correcting omissions such as no toe boards on scaffolds.
- About 20 percent of their time on safety training.
- The remaining 30 percent is spent on field inspections, record keeping, and finding and introducing new safety materials, techniques, and regulations.

Although Norton employs many safety professionals, their workforce is so large that their ratio of craft workers to safety professionals is 259.7 to 1—the next to highest in our very small sample. The long duration of each of their projects no doubt helps make this proportion of safety professionals effective by creating a situation that is similar to companies working in limited geographical areas, i.e., they keep workers on their projects for a much longer time than is true for most construction projects. Their good safety record is also attributable to their strong emphasis on safety planning and on safety training.

Combining Safety and Loss Control

In our small sample of five better-than-average companies, three companies give their safety professionals responsibility for insurance as well as safety: Yeats, Harris, and Hart and Johnson. These companies, like other construction companies recently, have moved away from the traditional exclusive focus on safety for their staffs.

More construction companies are deciding to combine safety and insurance responsibilities. Major reasons for this trend are the increased costs of workers' compensation and other insurance and the the need for a close monitoring of reserves in order to reduce their experience modification rating. To meet this growing career direction, more safety professionals are taking additional training in insurance management.

Summary

These six case studies demonstrate some of the varied ways in which safety professionals work with construction companies. They suggest that there is no one best way to organize the safety staff function in a construction company. There are many factors which need to be taken into account in deciding both on the size of the safety staff and on the particular activities which should be emphasized.

The first decision a construction company has to make is whether or not they want to hire at least one safety professional or rely solely on safety assistance from their insurance carrier or broker. As we mentioned earlier, more and more construction companies are finding that insurance costs make hiring their own safety professionals cost effective.

The number of safety professionals needed by a firm obviously varies with the total number of projects the company has under way at once and with the size and complexity of the projects, as well as with the total number of craft workers employed. The cases also bring out some other factors which can affect how large a safety staff is needed.

Let us assume that we are considering companies with equally high top management commitment and involvement in safety and in emphasis on supervisory accountability for safety performance. Their requirements for size of safety staff will still differ. A construction company which specializes in one type of construction has all its projects in one relatively limited geographical area, and typically uses a high proportion of the same supervisors and craft workers on its jobs year after year can obtain a good safety record with a smaller safety staff than can the same size company which takes on a large variety of different types of construction projects that are spread over a very wide geographical area using a high proportion of workers new to the company on each project.

The cases also bring out ways in which the duties of safety professionals correspond to the particular requirements of their companies, such as a higher emphasis on new-worker orientation and supervisory safety training when access to safety staff is more limited and when craft workers come to their jobs with less of a background in working safely. We also noted that construction companies are broadening the jobs of their safety professionals to cover insurance loss-control responsibilities.

Finding the best fit between the number and role of safety professionals and the characteristics of the company's construction projects is a task which has to be reviewed as conditions change. A company which maintains a size of staff and/or a definition of the role of their safety professionals based on assumptions about insurance costs and the types and conditions of work and workforce which are now outmoded may well find their safety record deteriorating and their insurance costs rising. Assessing safety staff size and role is a continuing responibility for both company management and those safety professionals working with them.

24

Summary of Action Steps for the Safety Professional

Reviewing the five previous chapters provides the following basic guidelines for safety professionals who want to help construction companies create excellent safety records.

Avoiding the Responsibility Trap

- Have as your fundamental goal the maintenance and strengthening of the responsibility and accountability of line managers for the safety records of their units.
- Encourage top management involvement in safety by appealing to the humanitarian and/or financial benefits of safety.
- Work with top management to develop safety accountability measures for line managers.
- Consider yourself a staff member who serves managers in the field.
- Teach line managers to become as aware of safety violations and unsafe actions as you are yourself—for example, take them around the site when you are making inspections so that they develop safety eyes.
- When jobs are too small to keep safety professionals on-site, encourage job-site managers to appoint job safety representatives.
- Be aware that your authority is based on (1) the societal need for safety in the workplace reflected in the OSHA laws, (2) construction safety expertise, (3) skill in working with people, and (4) top management support.
- Use logical persuasion rather than relying on directives to obtain line involvement.

- Improve your expertise by additional formal training, reading journals, and attending professional meetings.

- Increase your skill in working with people by taking courses in effective presentations, communication, and negotiating skills.

- Increase top management support by keeping top management informed and involved in ways that reinforce the idea of *line* responsibility for safety.

- Familiarize yourself with the details of construction so that your recommendations for changes will be practical and easy to understand.

- Keep line management informed of the latest laws about construction safety and the latest information on construction accidents and accidents in other relevant industries.

Buttressing Line Commitment

- Work with line management on developing effective orientation materials to reduce accidents in construction's most vulnerable group—new workers.

- Develop supervisory training courses and materials to use on the job—particularly on projects that have high proportions of new supervisors and workers.

- Frequently review project health and safety needs to determine when new training programs are required.

- Increase the effectiveness of toolbox meetings, provide information on job-relevant topics through a newsletter or checklists, and organize foremen planning groups or training sessions.

- Use job visits not only for monitoring the job for safety performance but also for informal training and for two-way communication with workers, foremen, and job-site managers on safety problems and solutions.

Selecting Safety Performance Measures

- Measure company safety performance by experience modification ratings and by OSHA recordable incident rate.

- Gauge company improvement by OSHA recordable incidence rate.

- Supervisory accountability for safety can be best served by an accident cost measure.

- Accident costs per employee hour supervised calculated on a monthly basis permit comparisons among all supervisors in one grouping such as job-site managers, general foremen, and foremen.

- OSHA reportable incidence can also be used effectively for supervisory accountability.

- Using lost-time accidents by themselves as an accountability measure is not recommended as it does not differentiate the safety records of job-site managers and foremen on a month-by-month basis.

- Categorizing accidents by part of body injured, type of injury, length of time worker is on the job, craft of injured worker, and in other ways can help locate areas needing improvement.

Working with Outside Groups

- Join the construction division of the American Society of Safety Engineers and the National Society for Safety Management to keep up to date on construction safety management.

- Represent your company on the safety committee of your contractor organization.

- Check the safety department of your national contractor organization for materials and programs.

- Utilize the consultation section of the state OSHA group, especially at the planning stage of a project.

- Check the state and national OSHA organizations for training programs and materials.

- Become acquainted with the staffs of safety and health professionals in the national and international organizations of the relevant building trade unions.

- Check your regional colleges and universities for safety management courses.

- Constantly be on the lookout for ideas from other groups which will strengthen the safety performance of the line managers with whom you work.

- Remember that there are many safety professionals working to improve construction safety performance; you don't have to reinvent the wheel; you can obtain help from others in solving your company's safety problems.

Finding the Best Fit

- Review the special needs of the job-site mangers, foremen, and workers for whom you are staff.

- Develop and expand orientation and training materials and programs when there is a high proportion of new workers and/or when there are changes in types and methods of work undertaken.

- Work with top management on an analysis of the needed support from safety professionals in order to maintain high project safety performance.

- In reviewing safety staff requirements, note that a higher proportion of safety staff to craft workers is generally needed when company projects are large, varied, geographically spread out, and depend primarily upon workers who have not previously worked for the company.

- Review the present handling of insurance loss control. In situations in which safety and insurance are handled separately, consider whether combining insurance loss-control responsibilities with safety in the job of safety professional would decrease company accident costs.

Buying Safe Construction

*For U.S. manufacturers struggling to compete in
international or domestic markets, reducing capital facility
costs in all ways possible can be a matter of survival.
Accidents cost the U.S. construction industry billions of
dollars annually. In the short term, these costs are absorbed
by contractors in the form of higher insurance premiums and
indirect costs. But they are ultimately passed on to
construction buyers in the form of higher reimbursable costs
or higher bids on future work. A Business Roundtable study
(Levitt et al., 1981; the Business Roundtable, 1982) has
determined that even on hard money projects, accidents result
in higher costs for construction buyers through delays and
potential third-party liability. Consequently, construction
buyers have a vital stake in controlling and minimizing the
costs of construction accidents.*

*Historically, their legal counsel have advised construction
buyers that a hands-off policy by the buyer in the area of
construction safety preserved the contractor's status as an
"independent contractor" and insulated the buyer from
liability for injuries to construction workers or third parties.
As a result, construction buyers have traditionally believed
that maintaining such a hands-off relationship with their
contractors in the area of safety was good practice.
Historically this may have been good legal advice. It is not
good advice today!*

*Recent cases in several states indicate that courts will no
longer hold construction buyers harmless against third-party*

lawsuits that result from construction accidents where buyers attempt to maintain a hands-off safety policy. Buyers have been found liable for construction injury claims even when they wrote "hold harmless" provisions into their construction contracts and scrupulously avoided any direction or guidance to contractors in matters dealing with safety.

A 1984 study of this subject found that prudent attempts by construction buyers to select safe contractors, to provide orientation materials or training for contractor employees, and to monitor site construction safety through devices such as permits or inspections is now more likely to reduce the buyer's liability for construction accidents (Koch, 1984). A previous study conducted for the Business Roundtable found that construction buyers who took active steps to select safe contractors and to monitor construction safety had fewer accidents on their projects than did less involved construction buyers in similar industries (Levitt et al., 1981; the Business Roundtable, 1982).

Even the most conservative corporate attorney will agree that reducing the frequency and severity of construction accidents is a good way to reduce the buyer's liability. There is now strong evidence which shows that proper involvement by construction buyers can reduce construction accidents without shifting liability to the buyer for those accidents that may still happen.

Considering the extremely high cost of construction accidents (documented in Part 1 of this book), construction buyers who are persuaded to follow the outdated approach of maintaining a hands-off policy in this area may be missing a significant opportunity to cut the cost of their capital facilities. For buyers who choose to get involved in managing construction safety costs, the next three chapters provide guidelines for selecting and controlling construction contractors to achieve enhanced safety performance on future capital projects.

This section is primarily aimed at organizations that buy construction services to provide their capital facilities: manufacturing or service companies, real estate developers, utilities, and the like. However, a general contractor that is subcontracting out part of its work to another firm is also a construction buyer. Many of the ideas presented in this part of the book can be used by general contractors or construction managers in dealing with specialty contractors on their projects.

25

Selecting Safe Contractors

Even the most crusty and conservative corporate counsel would have to agree that selecting contractors based upon their expected safety performance will not increase a buyer's liability for construction accidents. Moreover, it is an easy and proven effective method to enhance construction safety. We will, therefore, discuss safety selection before dealing with the slightly more controversial topic of monitoring contractor safety.

Oilco, a major oil company with an excellent record of safety on its construction sites, believes strongly that it can lower the cost of new capital facilities through aggressive screening of contractors by using their past safety performance. Oilco's safety director says: "We keep our own statistics on safety performance for all of the contractors' project managers who have worked on our projects in the past. When negotiating or bidding major new facilities, we request past safety data on all key project staff and analyze this data together with our own data. This is given considerable weight in short-listing contractors for a bid or in selecting contractors on negotiated jobs."

The Business Roundtable's (1982) popular A-3 report, *Improving Construction Safety Performance,* has contributed to a growing awareness by many construction buyers that selection of safer contractors can pay dividends. Increasingly, construction buyers are beginning to evaluate potential contractors' expected safety performance as another criterion for being permitted to bid or for being selected to work on their projects. Our research indicates that screening contractors in terms of their expected safety performance is an easy and effective way for construction buyers to reduce accident costs.

In this chapter we suggest that buyers consider including safety among the criteria for prequalification or selection of prospective contractors, and we give guidelines for doing so.

Who Should Evaluate Contractor Safety?

Our answer to this question is that all construction buyers should evaluate their prospective contractors' safety performance. And general contractors or construction manager (CM) firms should likewise evaluate the expected safety performance of prospective specialty contractors. Depending upon the nature of the contract award process and on the capabilities of the buyer's in-house staff, the timing and purpose of the safety evaluation will differ slightly.

Open or closed competitive bids

Many construction buyers, especially public agencies, award work based upon open competitive bids. Buyers using this contracting approach frequently require that all bidders submit a performance and payment surety bond as part of their bid package. This delegates the task of prequalifying contractors to surety firms' agents or brokers who are experienced at evaluating contractors' financial and technical soundness.

In case of a default by the prime contractor, surety bonding firms assume the obligation to complete the project and to pay any material suppliers or subcontractors with valid claims against the project. However, buyers should be aware that sureties accept no liability for third-party injury claims made against the buyer arising from construction accidents and are, therefore, not motivated by this risk. Consequently, few surety firms routinely investigate contractors' past safety records or current safety practices in any detail when deciding whether or not to furnish them surety bonds.

Many private construction buyers that award work by competitive bidding maintain their own closed bid lists and use their own staff and criteria to prequalify contractors for inclusion in these lists. Just like the sureties, many of these buyers do not currently ask for nor analyze data on contractors' safety history and practices.

We recommend that all construction buyers employing either open or closed competitive bidding collect the needed data from prospective bidders and exclude those whose past safety records and current safety practices indicate that it is likely that they will be unsafe.

In attempting to do this, each buyer will have to set its own limits of acceptability beyond which contractors will be excluded from bidding. For example, a buyer might decide that it wanted to exclude the least safe 5 percent of firms from bidding its work. Later in this chapter, we provide references to industry comparative data sources and examples of how such screening might be implemented.

At the same time, we recognize that excluding bidders—even suspected unsafe bidders—may be especially difficult for public agencies to do. Since most public agencies currently rely upon surety firms to do the screening for them, we recommend that they investigate possible contractual changes or other methods to get surety firms to take safety into account when evaluating contractors for bonds on their projects.

Competitive negotiation

When construction buyers award work based upon competitive negotiation, they typically solicit proposals from a limited number of firms that they consider well qualified to carry out the project. They develop a set of evaluation criteria representing desired characteristics of prospective contractors for the given project and assign weights to each criterion. Proposals are ranked in terms of their total scores, and the buyer attempts to negotiate with the top one or few firms.

We suggest that safety evaluation be part of this process, too. A buyer can use safety as a screen to exclude the least safe firms from even participating in the negotiation; and the buyer can give some weight to "expected safety performance" in the selection of the finalists. The guidelines which follow can be employed in both stages of the negotiation process.

Selecting specialty contractors

General contractors or construction managers (CMs) can employ the guidelines presented in this chapter when selecting specialty firms as subcontractors or prime contractors for their projects. Since general contractors and CM firms are increasingly being named in third-party lawsuits by specialty contractors' injured workers and since delays resulting from specialty contractors' accidents can cost them dearly, they have good reasons to exclude unsafe firms from working on their projects.

Factors to Consider in Safety Evaluation

The purpose of conducting a safety evaluation of a prospective contractor is to predict its expected safety performance on a future project. A safety evaluation for this purpose can be based upon two kinds of data:

1. Data about a contractor's *past safety record* provide an objective (although somewhat dated) prediction of its future performance;

these can be obtained from insurance measures, OSHA statistics, or references from past clients.

2. Data about the contractor's *current safety practices* provide a current, but more subjective, prediction of its future safety performance.

In the following sections we will discuss the use of both types of data in contractor prequalification or selection. A sample evaluation form which can be used as a starting point by construction buyers who wish to evaluate their prospective contractors' safety was developed by Stanford University under contract to the Business Roundtable (Levitt et al., 1981). The sample questionnaire is contained in Appendix A of this book; guidelines for its use are provided in Appendix B.

Data on past safety performance

In conducting our research on construction safety over the years, we have investigated many different measures of safety performance for differentiating between safe and less safe contractors. We believe that a contractor's experience modification rating (EMR) for workers' compensation insurance, although not a perfect measure, is nevertheless the single best measure of safety performance.

Experience modification rating. A contractor's EMR is the *ratio* of the firm's *actual workers' compensation insurance claims costs* to the firm's *expected workers compensation losses for its type of work,* averaged over *the oldest 3 of the last 4 years.* The advantage of this measure is that it is the most difficult for a contractor to manipulate. State rating bureaus use premium and claim data supplied by insurance carriers to compute each employer's EMR. The age of the data used in the computation (2 to 4 years) is the only major weakness of the EMR in predicting future safety performance (see Chapter 21 for a detailed discussion of this topic). In some states, such as California, the EMR is considered a matter of public record and may be obtained directly from the state insurance rating bureau. In other states it is not and must be provided by the contractor or its insurance carrier.

OSHA incidence rate. A firm's OSHA incidence rate, on the other hand, is available at the end of each year for the year just completed. It counts the number of OSHA reportable injuries (roughly equivalent to injuries requiring attention by a doctor) per 200,000 manhours. OSHA publishes guidelines for reporting these injuries and requires that contractors do so on a log sheet each year. Larger firms will often staff major projects with paramedics to provide faster attention for injured workers, and this can distort the numbers of doctor cases somewhat. On the other hand, smaller firms may be lax in recording all of their injuries since OSHA can not police these records thoroughly. Thus, OSHA reportable injuries are a more timely, albeit less objective, measure of past safety performance. Each contractor's OSHA incidence rates must be posted at its job sites, and this information is, therefore, not proprietary. Contractors should have no problem providing a prospective client with this information.

References from past clients.   Many construction buyers request that prospective contractors provide them with the names of past clients as references. In addition to asking previous clients for data about accidents or claims, these buyers typically ask previous clients questions such as whether the contractor maintained a clean job site and whether the contractor cooperated with the client's own safety personnel and programs.

We recommend that buyers ask prospective contractors to provide them with data on both EMR and OSHA reportable injuries and then give weight to each in their evaluation. If a contractor's performance is changing over time, the OSHA incidence rates for the most recent years should indicate the current direction of change. Furthermore, if a construction buyer has the resources to do so, seeking references from past clients is an excellent way to get additional information on a contractor's past safety record and practices.

Question 1 on the sample questionnaire in Appendix A requests data on the contractor's interstate EMR. If this is unavailable, the firm's intrastate EMR for the state in which the project will be built or for the firm's home state are acceptable substitutes (see Chapter 1 for a definition and discussion of each type of EMR). Questions 2, 3, and 4 of the sample questionnaire gather the data necessary to evaluate the contractor's OSHA incidence rate.

When a construction buyer is selecting the contractor for a major project through a proposal review procedure, the buyer may also want to evaluate the past safety performance of each of the key personnel proposed by each firm. Since EMRs are computed on a companywide basis and cannot be measured at the project level, *accident claims costs per workhour* or *OSHA incidence rates* for projects which key personnel have recently managed would be appropriate data on which to base such an evaluation. Question 10 of the sample questionnaire addresses this type of evaluation. Evaluation of the past safety performance of individuals is an area in which references by past clients of the contractor can be especially helpful.

Data on current safety practices

Part 2 of this book describes companywide safety policies and practices for construction firms that have been proven to be effective in reducing accidents. The remaining questions in the sample questionnaire (in Appendix A) were designed to obtain the most objective possible data to determine the extent to which a contractor is employing these proven effective safety practices. A high score on these questions indicates that the contractor's senior management has taken steps to provide an organizational setting in which safe construction is promoted.

Of course this data is far more subjective and should be treated with healthy skepticism by construction buyers. We recommend asking for documentation wherever appropriate. For instance, when asking about the frequency of accident cost or frequency reports sent to management, ask for the copies of the last two such reports for a representative number of projects.

One advantage of including this more subjective data on safety practices in the evaluation is that it is more current than the EMR. A firm may have recently instituted steps to improve its safety management practices and be on the way to improved safety performance, but the EMR will lag this change by 2 to 4 years.

We will review some of the key safety practices covered by the sample questionnaire in Appendix A:

- *Accountability for accidents.* Questions 5, 8, and 9 gather data to determine whether senior managers in the firm have established an accountability system under which supervisors at all levels are held accountable for their subordinates' accidents. Lists of accidents or claims costs totaled for each supervisor provide objective evidence that such an accountability system might exist. Without some compilation of this sort it cannot.

- *Safety training.* As discussed in Chapter 4, thorough training of new hires and new supervisors is a very effective way to reduce accidents. Questions 12 and 13 address worker and foremen training. Asking for examples of training materials would provide objective evidence in support of these questions and would be appropriate to do when evaluating contractors for a major project.

- *Formal safety program.* A contractor who has taken the trouble to develop a written statement of its safety program to hand out to all employees is demonstrating a concern for safety. Question 11 addresses this.

- *Safety meetings.* Toolbox safety meetings are required by law in many states. Contractors who can show evidence of carefully planned and documented toolbox meetings and/or meetings for site supervisors are likely to be safer. Questions 6 and 14 ask about the frequency of such meetings. Sample meeting materials or minutes would provide objective evidence that such meetings are taken seriously and might be the basis for additional points in a detailed selection process.

Assigning weights and cutoff limits

The sample safety evaluation questionnaire presented in Appendix A does not contain weights for each of the factors. The guidelines for its use in Appendix B show suggested weights, but these are only one possible alternative. Each buyer should decide which questions to include in its evaluation form and should assign weights to the factors according to its own desired emphasis. We suggest that the EMR and OSHA incidence rate data carry the highest weights, with EMR data weighed more heavily; data on accountability and training should have the next highest weights; and data on formal safety programs and meetings should have the lowest weights.

The same is true for cutoff limits. The sample questionnaire guidelines show distribution curves for EMR and OSHA incidence rates among firms. Each buyer must decide what it can accept. To illustrate, let us say that a buyer decides that it wishes to exclude any firm in the worst 10 percent of the distribution for EMRs or in the worst 20 percent of the distribution for OSHA incidence rates in its type of work. Using these cutoff limits, a building contractor with a California EMR above 1.5 or an OSHA incidence rate above about 33 would be excluded.

Buyers wishing to make a cutoff in this manner based on EMRs can use our data (in Appendix B) showing the distribution of EMRs if they are unable to obtain more current distributions, since these are not generally available. We have collected interstate and California EMRs on two separate occasions 10 years apart and have not observed significant variations in the distribution of EMR values.

To set cutoffs for OSHA incidence rates in each type of construction, buyers can consult the most recent OSHA incidence rate statistics (published every few years by the Bureau of Labor Statistics and available through regional OSHA offices).

Computerizing Safety Evaluation

A computer program called Safequal (1986) has been developed by one of the authors to assist construction buyers in evaluating the expected safety performance of contractors. We describe it here as an illustration of how the safety evaluation process can be automated.

A prequalification or selection questionnaire, similar to the one in Appendix A of this book, is provided with Safequal. This questionnaire is sent to each bidder or prospective contractor with the bid or proposal documents. The contractor completes this questionnaire and submits it along with its bid or proposal.

In conducting the safety evaluation, Safequal prompts the user for the answers to each of the questions on the questionnaire. At any stage of the data entry process, Safequal can provide the user with on-line assistance in using the program and with explanations which clarify or expand upon the questions and their possible answers. These on-line help and explanation facilities rapidly train the user's data entry person in the significance of each factor being considered and assist in entering the correct values.

After a contractor's responses have been entered, the program computes the contractor's overall score on the evaluation. If any of the contractor's answers fall outside of the acceptable ranges established by the buyer, the program will state that the contractor is unacceptable and will explain why. A permanent record of each evaluation can be saved on disk or printed during the evaluation. Since Safequal was based on the same Business Roundtable study as the sample questionnaire in this book, it follows our recommended content and weightings for factors very closely.

A companion program, Howsafe (1986), provides an in-depth diagnosis of a contractor's organization and procedures and makes recommendations for needed changes to improve safety performance. Safequal and Howsafe are currently supported on IBM and compatible personal computers.

A construction buyer can use an off-the-shelf package such as Safequal without modification, adapt it as desired, or develop its own program of this type. The benefits of computerizing a safety evaluation in this way are:

- *Consistency.* All contractors will be evaluated using the same factors and weights.

- *Completeness.* A program such as this acts as an "intelligent checklist" to ensure that items are not omitted.

- *Accuracy.* Computational errors are eliminated by such a system.

Summary

In the past many construction buyers have felt that maintaining a hands-off policy in the area of construction safety protected them from liability for construction injuries. Current case law indicates that this is no longer so. If construction buyers wish to reduce accident costs but do not wish to inspect or monitor construction operations, selecting contractors based upon their expected safety performance is an easy and proven effective manner to achieve this goal.

In this chapter we have suggested how safety selection can be factored into several different kinds of bidding or negotiation processes. A sample safety questionnaire, along with guidelines for its use have been included as Appendix A and Appendix B of this book. Finally we discussed Safequal, an example of a computer program which has been developed to assist construction buyers in evaluating or prequalifying contractors based upon their expected safety performance.

Chapter

26

Monitoring Contractor Safety

> The project manager of a refinery expansion project for a large petrochemical company with an outstanding safety record told us, "Our construction contract requires that contractors follow our safety requirements and gives us the right to terminate their contracts if they do not. The first time we caught the reinforcing steel contractor driving its truck too fast in a designated 10-mph zone through our site we gave them a stern warning. A week later one of its drivers was speeding again. We terminated the firm's contract on the spot. We lost a few days on some noncritical activities, but the other contractors on the site sure got the message!"

The true situation described above is typical of the attitudes which we found in a study of construction buyers whose firms had outstanding safety performance on their construction projects (Levitt et al., 1981). In some cases these firms had already attempted to screen out the least safe contractors through prequalification; in others, they relied only on monitoring during construction to control accidents. In all cases they stated that they believed that active involvement in construction safety, done properly, served to reduce rather than increase their firm's potential liability for construction accidents. This chapter describes the techniques used by the safest construction buyers to manage construction safety on their projects.

Involvement Pays Dividends

The first point we want to make is that involvement by the buyer in construction safety pays off in terms of reduced accidents. Data from the Business Roundtable's study (Levitt et al., 1981; the Business Roundtable, 1982) demonstrate this convincingly. In this study buyers were asked to list the methods they employed (if any) to monitor construction contractors on their projects. There were a number of significant differences between the actions taken by safe and less safe buyers. We have listed the actions in order of significance:

1. *Stress safety as part of the contract during prejob walk-around.* This gives contractors the opportunity to include all safety-related items in their bids and lets contractors know early that the buyer is serious about safety.

2. *Require short-term permits, rather than ongoing permits, for hazardous activities.* This means that contractors must check daily or more frequently to ensure that any planned hazardous activities are coordinated with other contractors and with the buyer's own plant workforce.

3. *Conduct safety audits of the contractor during construction.* The buyer's or construction manager's safety staff conduct these audits to ensure compliance with the buyer's safety requirements and all state and federal safety regulations. They are aimed at systems and procedures rather than at specific hazards.

4. *Conduct periodic safety inspections.* This is to ensure that the contractors are controlling physical safety hazards on their parts of the projects. This complements item 3 above.

5. *Weigh safety in prequalifying contractors for the bid.* Relatively few buyers in our survey did this, but those that did were among the safest firms in the industry.

6. *Require safety training of contractors' employees.* Buyers may be more knowledgeable than their contractors about the hazards associated with certain types of work on their facilities. Even when this is not the case, ensuring that contractors provide safety training for all new employees will help to avoid injuries to the most vulnerable construction workers.

7. *Maintain statistics of the contractor's safety performance.* These statistics can provide the basis for dividend sharing (described in the following chapter) as well as for selecting contractors on future work.

8. *Set goals for construction safety.* Projectwide safety goals should be set, along with specific goals for contractors who need special attention because of past poor performance or particularly hazardous work operations.

9. *Set safety guidelines into the body of the contract.* By safety

guidelines we mean more than a single paragraph requiring the contractor to conform with state and federal regulations. We mean several pages of specific required procedures or actions that constitute minimum acceptable practices in the area of safety that all contractors must follow on a particular project.

10. *Set up a construction safety department to monitor contractor safety.* Most buyers in our survey had one or more construction safety specialists in their corporate industrial safety departments. A few had special departments for construction safety.

11. *Require immediate reporting of contractor accidents.* Immediate rather than periodic reporting gives the buyer or its agent more time to intervene and ensure that the contractor has corrected any identified hazard before others can be injured by it. Such notification can also serve to involve the contractor's senior management if necessary.

12. *Discuss safety at owner-contractor meetings.* Past safety performance of the contractor, special hazards involved in upcoming work, and interface safety issues are appropriate items to discuss at such meetings.

13. *Provide contractors with safety guidelines they must follow.* Any site specific procedures such as emergency travel routes, evacuation procedures, special hazards, etc., are covered in these guidelines.

14. *Investigate the contractors' accidents.* The buyer's involvement in investigating the contractors' accidents gives the client valuable insights about generic safety hazards on the project, as well as additional insight into the contractors' organization and capabilities in the area of safety.

15. *Require the contractor to designate safety responsibility to someone on site.* If the contractor does not have a safety professional on the site, this step requires that the contractor assign a line manager to coordinate safety matters. The responsibility for safety, of course, always remains with line managers.

In our survey, buyers were classified into two groups: those with known excellent safety records, and "average" construction buyers whose construction safety records were unknown. When we compared these two groups we found that:

- Buyers exhibited a considerable range of involvement in construction safety, from almost none to a great deal.
- The extremely safe buyers used most of the safety management techniques listed above, while the average buyers used few if any of them.

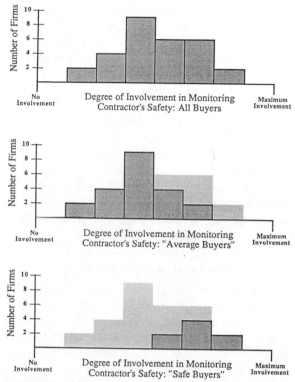

Figure 26.1 Effect of buyer monitoring on construction safety. (SOURCE: *Adapted from R. E. Levitt, H. W. Parker, and N. M. Samelson, "Improving Construction Safety Performance: The User's Role,"* Technical Report No. 260, 2nd ed., *Department of Civil Engineering, Stanford University, August 1985 pp. 39–40.)*

Figure 26.1 illustrates this point. We gave the construction buyers points for the degree to which they employed each of these 15 techniques on their projects and then plotted a histogram of their scores. This is shown in the first histogram in Figure 26.1. Note that degrees of involvement are distributed all the way from almost no involvement with the technique to employing virtually all of the listed techniques.

Then we separated the buyers into the average group versus the extremely safe group. These are shown in the second and third histograms. Note that the safest construction buyers are all near the top end of the scale in terms of their involvement in contractor safety.

In addition to the areas listed above, buyers should consider involvement in two areas whose importance has grown since the Business Roundtable study was completed:

- Federal and state "right to know" laws now place stringent obligations on employers to inform their workers about identification and handling of potentially hazardous materials in the workplace. Buyers must require that contractors provide them with a list of any hazardous materials that will be brought onto the job site, along with storage dispensing and clean-up procedures for each of these substances.

  Buyers must provide contractors with the same type of information about hazardous substances used or stored in and around their operating facilities where contractors will be required to work. Buyers must also alert contractors to the presence of hazardous materials in underground storage tanks or of hazardous wastes buried in landfills to which contractors' workers may be exposed and must identify proper personal protective equipment and other handling procedures for such materials. This is an area in which the buyer clearly has superior knowledge to most contractors, so the courts will not allow a buyer to maintain a hands-off policy.

- Alcohol and drug abuse are of growing concern to all employers. Measures to be taken for screening workers (which may be difficult or impossible under some construction labor agreements) and for identifying and dealing with workers suspected of being under the influence of alcohol or drugs on the job must be clarified and agreed upon with contractors before they commence work.

  Some construction buyers have become very aggressive in this area, requiring drug screening as a condition of hiring for construction workers on their projects. In one case, the result was a dramatic increase in productivity, along with reductions in absenteeism and accidents.

Some of the extremely safe buyers in the Business Roundtable study did not prequalify or select contractors based upon their past safety records. Rather, they relied on strong monitoring strategies to achieve this performance. The Business Roundtable study, therefore, provides strong evidence that construction buyers who choose to become actively involved in monitoring the safety performance of their contractors can obtain excellent safety performance even from average contractors.

The Business Roundtable data also serve to reinforce the point that construction safety provides a significant opportunity for construction buyers to improve the cost effectiveness of their capital expansion programs. Of the $10 billion in potential annual cost savings for construction identified in 23 separate areas of the Business Roundtable's Construction Industry Cost Effectiveness Project (the Business Roundtable, 1984), almost 30 percent or $3 billion of potential annual savings came from one area—improved construction safety performance!

Respecting the Contractor's Independence

In implementing these safety monitoring techniques, the safest construction buyers are careful to respect the contractor's independence. Contractual provisions cause no problems here, but permits, safety inspections, and meetings could be problematic. *These buyers are careful to work through the contractor's chain of supervision at all times,* dealing with foremen, superintendents, or the contractor's designated safety representatives. *They scrupulously avoid giving direct instructions to the contractor's craft workers except in the event of a work practice or situation which they deem to be one of imminent danger* and which needs to be corrected on the spot.

Some buyers have expressed concern about enforcing a particular work method during construction when this method was not specified in the original contract. If a contractor can show that its bid for a project was based upon using a different work method which was permissable under state or federal OSHA regulations, the buyer could be held to have imposed a "constructive change" on the contractor. In this case, the buyer could be required to pay any difference in the contractor's cost for using the required method. This is seldom a major issue in practice but may arise infrequently. The prejob safety walk-around with the contractor is the time to discuss proposed work methods for hazardous operations and to resolve any ambiguities of this type.

Provided that these two cautions are exercised, the construction buyers in our study felt that their liability for construction accidents is not increased by active safety monitoring and might actually be reduced. A subsequent study of the issue of third-party liability for construction accidents carried out by James Koch (1983) adds additional weight to this view.

Maintenance or Plant Expansion Projects

Some of the buyers in our study stated that they provided increased safety monitoring for projects that involved maintenance or expansion of existing operating facilities. First, they stated that their maintenance contractors were often smaller, less sophisticated operators who needed more assistance in this area than did the contractors on their new construction projects. Second, they explained that increased levels of monitoring on maintenance or expansion projects were justified by the risk of injury to their own plant employees and by the large potential cost impact of any interruption to the existing plant's output in the event of a construction accident.

Selecting versus Monitoring for Safety

Our study found that extremely safe construction buyers used selection, monitoring, or both strategies.

Watt, a very safe electric utility, is unable to provide monitoring on many of its projects which are small and far from the firm's headquarters. For such projects, the company relies strictly on prequalification to eliminate unsafe contractors.

Gusher, a major oil company which participated in our survey, also relies primarily on selection to manage its plant construction safety. This firm maintains data for all of its past projects on the safety records of individual project managers employed by each of its contractors. When selecting firms for new work, the company asks contractors for the names of key project personnel and consults its records. If the manager has not previously worked on one of its projects, the company asks for information on the manager's past safety performance on projects for other buyers.

Other firms reported that they relied primarily on monitoring to manage construction safety.

Black Gold, another oil company with an equally outstanding record of construction safety, does not eliminate firms with unsafe records from its bid list. However, it asks for contractors' EMR data and is thus alerted to potential problems. If this buyer identifies a contractor with a poor safety record, it watches the contractor extra carefully. By insisting upon thorough safety orientation, permits for hazardous work, and safety inspections, all supported by strong contractual provisions, this buyer has obtained an enviable record of construction safety.

Others among the list of extremely safe buyers in our study employ some safety selection in which they eliminate extremely unsafe firms, but they also rely on monitoring to maintain safety standards on their job sites.

We recommend that construction buyers ask for information about the past safety performance and current safety practices of their prospective contractors in all cases. Wherever legally or politically possible we urge buyers to use safety prequalification or selection as the cheapest and least invasive means to reduce construction accidents. If technical capability or market conditions require a construction buyer to employ a contractor with a known poor safety record, aggressive monitoring strategies as described in this chapter can ensure that safety performance will be controlled on site.

Summary

We presented data from a major study of the construction buyer's role in safety management. These data show that buyers can be actively involved in monitoring contractor safety while respecting the contractor's legal independence and that such monitoring pays off in improved safety performance. Examples of the monitoring techniques used by extremely safe construction buyers are presented throughout the chapter. Results from this study and from a more recent one suggest that, in so doing, buyers will not increase their liability for construction accidents—and may actually reduce it—so long as they respect the contractor's chain of supervision.

27

Guidelines for Using Wrap-Up Insurance

On a number of large projects that were completed during the last decade, the project's buyer elected to furnish all construction-related insurance. The use of such buyer-furnished or wrap-up insurance has often led to confusion and ill-feeling among both the buyer and contractors involved. We include a brief chapter on this subject to attempt to clarify the nature and purpose of wrap-up insurance and to suggest guidelines for construction buyers planning to furnish insurance for their construction contractors.

What Is Wrap-Up Insurance?

Wrap-up or owner-furnished insurance is an arrangement under which the buyer of a construction project furnishes all or part of the required insurance for all contractors on the project. Types of insurance that may be purchased under a wrap-up policy include workers' compensation, builders' risk, and liability. In addition more specialized types of coverage (such as railroad protective insurance for a subway project which will be constructed underneath the tracks of an operating railroad) may be purchased under the same umbrella.

Under a wrap-up policy, the construction buyer pays all insurance premiums for the types of coverage included in the policy. The EMR used in determining the premiums for workers' compensation insurance, by far the most expensive type of coverage, is negotiated. It may simply be the book rate (i.e., 100 percent) or it may be an average of the EMRs for the major contractors, weighted by their expected payroll on the project. In some cases, the buyer's insurance carrier writes individual workers' compensation policies with each contractor on the project, using the contractors' current EMR. In virtually all cases the buyer, as the payer of the premiums, receives the dividends for better than expected safety performance by contractors on the project.

The buyer informs contractors during the bidding or negotiating stage of the project that it plans to furnish certain types of construction insurance for the project. Contractors are informed that they should suspend their own coverage in these areas for the given project and remove these insurance costs from their bids.

Since it will be providing the insurance coverage, the buyer typically takes on the administration of the loss-control and safety management functions normally carried out by contractors' safety personnel or insurance loss-control consultants.

Pros and Cons of Using Wrap-Up Insurance

Wrap-up insurance, if used intelligently, can have advantages for the buyer of a large and complex project. Some of the major reasons for using it are discussed in this section, along with some unintended and often overlooked disadvantages.

Eliminating cross-liability suits

On large industrial or infrastructure projects, there may be several prime contractors working simultaneously (versus one prime contractor and its subcontractors). Moreover, none of the prime contractors has direct authority to manage or control the work of the others since they are all prime contractors with the buyer. In this situation, unsafe acts by employees of one firm can result in injuries to employees of another. The cross liability for accidents of this type can lead to a flurry of lawsuits between the insurance carriers of the two prime contractors, with neither one wishing to pay for the loss. Eventually, after the dust settles, one or both of them will have to pay up. In the meantime, site managers get tied up in the legal proceedings and morale and productivity can be severely eroded on the project.

If the two firms in question happen to be covered by the same carrier, there is no reason for the carrier to sue itself. It has to pay up, no matter who was at fault. So work on the project continues without the lawsuit that might otherwise have arisen. Elimination of such lawsuits is a key reason for the buyer of a major project to consider the use of wrap-up insurance.

Of course, injured workers are still free to try to recover damages in tort for injuries suffered on construction projects. As described in Chapter 26, they are now often suing third-party contractors and the project's buyer for additional sums even where cases are clearly covered by workers' compensation insurance. When wrap-up insurance is in place, the buyer and its construction manager are in the direct line of fire for such third party lawsuits. A $500,000,000 lawsuit of this type was narrowly defeated (on a technicality) in 1984 by the construction manager for a major mass transit project.

Thus, although wrap-up insurance does eliminate many bothersome cross-liability suits between contractors on the same project, it is not a panacea for liability suits.

Standardization of project safety procedures

In the absence of a single general contractor with responsibility for the general conditions on a job site, it can be tempting for multiple prime contractors to try to avoid the costs of adequate cleanup and to let those that follow behind them bear this expense. At the same time, specialty contractors in fields such as insulation, painting or steel erection may have their own well-developed safety programs. Conflicts between the standards imposed by a projectwide safety coordinator and their own procedures can be confusing and dangerous.

Thus, the safety of the overall job site needs to be coordinated by the project's buyer or by the firm hired to be its construction manager. Achieving uniform, projectwide safety standards is a potential advantage of wrap-up insurance, but it requires aggressive action by the buyer's safety staff or by the safety staff of its CM for the project.

Economies of scale

Insurance carriers or brokers make a convincing claim to project buyers that wrap-up insurance affords economies of scale in the purchase and administration of insurance coverage for the project. Since the insurance costs on a major project are large, small percentage savings represent large sums.

Wrap-up insurance may afford some economies of scale, but buyers should be aware that temporarily suspending (and subsequently reinstating) their own insurance coverage is an administrative headache for contractors on a wrap-up project. Moreover, removing the premiums for a major project from their insurance accounts reduces each contractor's economies of scale in purchasing its own insurance for other projects. For these two reasons, many of the second or third tier specialty subcontractors will often end up continuing their own coverage on wrap-up projects even though this duplicates the coverage purchased by the project's buyer.

Ultimately, buyers who elect to use wrap-up insurance must pay for these hidden administrative and market costs incurred by their contractors, so the actual savings in premiums may be smaller than they appear to be.

Dividends accruing to the buyer

As explained in Chapter 1, workers' compensation insurance is often sold under a dividend plan. Carriers who sell wrap-up insurance coverage almost always incorporate this type of self-insurance in which the buyer will receive a refund or dividend if actual losses are below the expected or target levels. Once again, the numbers are large and the dividends can amount to millions of dollars. Buyers' project managers and insurance or safety staff are delighted to have the opportunity to earn these dividends which can be presented to their top management at the end of the year with great fanfare.

The disadvantage of this is that contractors thereby lose their motivation to earn a dividend based on their own safety performance. Their accidents are still figured into their firms' experience modification ratings (EMRs), but as discussed in Chapter 1, the EMR is often too vague and distant an outcome to motivate job-site managers over the duration of a single project. Consequently, contractors' job-site managers lose an important incentive for safe construction when the buyer receives all of the dividends for projectwide safety perfomance.

Furthermore, contractors lose the ability to monitor their workers' compensation reserves under wrap-up insurance since the insurance contract is between the buyer and the carrier. Hence, many construction firms have developed a strong aversion to this form of insurance and may reflect it in higher prices for their work.

Insurance market reasons

Insurance markets for large risks are currently in turmoil. As a result, desired levels of liability insurance or special coverages such as railroad protective insurance may be very difficult to find for some projects. Pooling the risks—and premiums—for a major project has sometimes been the only way that the buyer can obtain the desired types and levels of coverage. At least one major U.S. subway construction project elected to use wrap-up insurance coverage for this reason.

Buyers who elect to use wrap-up insurance under market pressures, rather than because they themselves have superior safety management and risk control capabilities, should be especially careful to pay for and get adequate levels of safety management and loss-control services from the CM firms that they hire to manage their projects.

Guidelines for Using Wrap-Up Insurance

For some major projects, the advantages of wrap-up insurance may outweigh the disadvantages and buyers may choose to provide insurance. Analysis of experience from several projects for which wrap-up insurance was used suggests some actions that buyers can take when using wrap-up coverage to maximize the benefits and minimize the costs of doing so.

1. *Get involved in safety management.* Since tort settlements are so much larger than workers' compensation settlements, injured workers will be encouraged to seek additional compensation under tort claims against the project's owner or construction manager. Even when wrap-up insurance is in place, the buyer remains in the direct line of fire for such lawsuits. Adequate levels of liability insurance to cover such claims are becoming ever more costly and difficult to obtain, so the only sure defense against liability for the project's buyer is to have fewer accidents.

An arm's length relationship is no longer a defense against third-party lawsuits by injured construction workers. Consequently, we recommend that the buyer or its agent screen firms prior to an award to eliminate, or at least identify, firms with poor safety records. We further suggest that the buyer or construction manager monitor the operations of such potentially unsafe contractors as described in the previous chapter. In addition, the buyer or its agent should coordinate safety issues of a projectwide nature and hazards at the interfaces between tasks and work areas of different contractors to ensure that these do not get overlooked.

If neither the buyer nor the construction manager has the staff to carry out this function, then suitably qualified safety professionals must be employed for the duration of the project. The way to minimize the buyer's liability (and construction cost) is to minimize accidents.

2. *Communicate to avoid double coverage.* The buyer or construction manager should clearly inform all contractors and subcontractors on the project of the coverages and limits for which it will purchase wrap-up insurance. This will enable contractors to fill any gaps in desired coverage, and it should eliminate much of the double coverage. Nevertheless, buyers should expect that some firms will be unable or unwilling to temporarily suspend their own insurance coverage and will provide duplicate coverage anyway.

3. *Share dividends with safe contractors.* When the wrap-up policy has a dividend plan, we strongly encourage buyers to follow the example of the Washington D.C. Metro authority and to share the dividends with those contractors on the project that experience better than average safety performance. One contractor on the Washington D.C. Metro project received a dividend check for almost $500,000. And the buyer saved an equal amount or more through reduced accident costs and delays and through improved morale on the project.

As mentioned previously, contractors still have their accidents included in their EMR computations, but this is a remote incentive and should be augmented, where possible, by a dividend-sharing plan on the project. Buyers who attempt to retain all of the dividends under a wrap-up policy could be paying a high price for a short-term gain.

28

Summary of
the Buyer's Role

The Business Roundtable estimates that almost $3 billion can be saved annually by commercial and industrial construction buyers through improved construction safety performance. If maintaining a hands-off policy in the area of construction safety was ever a good strategy for construction buyers, it no longer is today. Several recent studies confirm that appropriate involvement by construction buyers in selecting and monitoring construction contractors and in designing insurance and loss-control programs for their major projects can help to reduce accidents.

In today's legal environment, taking the necessary steps to reduce the number of construction accidents is the only sure way for buyers to limit their liability exposure in this area. In this part of the book, we have set out proven effective guidelines for construction buyers to follow in selecting and monitoring construction contractors on their projects and in furnishing wrap-up insurance and loss-control services for their major projects.

Selecting Safe Contractors

Whereas some conservative attorneys might still balk at active monitoring of construction contractors, few will suggest that selecting contractors based upon their expected safety performance can increase the buyer's liability for any construction accidents that may still occur. And experience shows that it helps to reduce accidents.

1. Prequalify contractors to bid—gather the necessary data to screen out contractors whose expected safety performance is unacceptable.

    a. Use data on past safety performance, including the experience modification rating (EMR), the OSHA incidence rate, and references by past clients where available.

    b. Use data on current safety practices—Appendix A of this book contains a sample questionnaire for gathering such data.

2. Use expected safety performance as a selection criterion when negotiating awards—gather the same type of data as for prequalification, score the evaluation, and give it significant weight in the overall selection process.

3. Consider automating the safety evaluation process—automating the process provides consistent, complete, and accurate evaluations.

    a. Safequal, a computer program for automating the safety evaluation procedure, is one attempt to do this.

    b. Buyers can use such a program as is, customize it with their own weights and cutoff limits, or develop a computerized process independently.

Monitoring Contractor Safety

Some construction buyers, especially governmental agencies, may find it difficult or undesirable to screen out unsafe contractors through a selection process. Since the courts will no longer regard absence of involvement by the buyer as a shield against liability—in fact the contrary now appears to be the case—all construction buyers have an incentive to monitor construction safety on their projects. A recent study by the Business Roundtable (1982) confirms this and shows strong evidence that actively involved buyers have fewer accidents on their projects.

1. The safest construction buyers take the following steps on their projects (in order of frequency reported):

    a. Stress safety concerns during prejob walk-around.

    b. Require short-term permits for hazardous activities.

    c. Conduct audits of contractors' safety management procedures.

    d. Conduct periodic safety inspections.

    e. Weigh safety in prequalifying contractors.

    f. Require safety training of contractors' employees.

    g. Maintain statistics on contractors' safety performance.

    h. Set goals for safety performance.

    i. Set safety guidelines into the body of the contract.

    j. Set up a construction safety department.

    k. Require immediate reporting of accidents.

    l. Discuss safety at buyer-contractor meetings.

    m. Provide the contractor with safety guidelines.
    n. Investigate contractors' accidents.
    o. Require contractors to designate safety responsibility.

2. In addition to these practices of safe buyers reported in the Business
   Roundtable (1982) study, two additional areas have recently assumed more prominence and are suggested as potential areas of
   involvement for concerned buyers:
   a. State and federal right-to-know legislation has created new
       reporting requirements for hazardous materials in the work-
       place; buyers should have contractors list all hazardous materi-
       als brought to the workplace and should provide contractors with
       a list of known hazardous materials at an operating plant,
       including liquids in underground tanks or hazardous wastes
       buried in landfills.
   b. Alcohol and drug abuse has become more of a concern recently;
       buyers should consider appropriate levels of involvement in pre-
       employment screening of workers, supervisor training, and re-
       habilitation programs. Several buyers who have chosen to be-
       come involved in this area have seen big paybacks in productiv-
       ity as well as in safety.

In all of these areas, buyers should be careful to respect the
independence of the contractor by working through the contractor's
chain of supervision. Direct instructions to a contractor's field labor
force should be avoided except in cases of imminent danger.

Guidelines for Using Wrap-up Insurance

Wrap-up or buyer-furnished insurance has been used on a number of
major projects in recent years. Insurance brokers are usually familiar
with the advantages of this type of arrangement for construction
insurance, but the approach has certain drawbacks which should be
understood by buyers. In cases in which the advantages outweigh the
disadvantages, guidelines are provided for setting up such a program
to maximize its advantages.

- *Get involved in safety management.* Wrap-up insurance does not
  protect a construction buyer from liability for construction accidents.
  In fact, the buyer has a special responsibility under wrap-up insurance to provide overall safety coordination on a job-site. If the buyer
  does not have adequate staff to carry out this function, it must be
  performed by the construction manager or the buyer must contract
  separately for these services.
- *Communicate to avoid double coverage.* Contractors and especially
  subcontractors must be informed of the types and levels of coverage

furnished under the wrap-up arrangement. This will minimize, but will seldom eliminate, double coverage by contractors who choose not to suspend their own coverage or who are unaware of the buyer-furnished insurance.

- *Share dividends with the safer contractors.*   Many buyers choose to keep all of the workers' compensation insurance dividends generated under a wrap-up plan rather than sharing them with the safer contractors whose good safety performance earned the dividend. This is a short-sighted policy which can be costly to the buyer as contractors will be less motivated to be safe.

Items for Inclusion in Contractor Safety Evaluation Questionnaire

1. List your firm's Interstate Experience Modification Rate for the last 3 years:
   198 _____   198 _____   198 _____

2. Please use your last year's OSHA no. 200 log to fill in:
   Number of injuries and illnesses:
   (*a*) number of lost workday cases _____
   (*b*) number of restricted workday cases _____
   (*c*) number of cases with medical attention only _____
   (*d*) number of fatalities _____

3. Employee hours worked last year (do not include any nonwork time, even though paid) _____

4. Check your type of work: Nonresidential building _____
                           Heavy (nonhighway) construction _____
                       Plumbing, heating, and air conditioning _____
                                              Other _____

5. Are accident reports (OSHA 200) and report summaries sent to the following? How often?

	No	Yes	Monthly	Quarterly	Annually
Field superintendent	___	___	___	___	___
Vice president of construction	___	___	___	___	___
President of firm	___	___	___	___	___

6. Do you hold site safety meetings for field supervisors?
   Yes _____ No _____ How often? Weekly _____ Biweekly _____
   Monthly _____ Less often, as needed _____

(Continued)

7. Do you conduct project safety inspections? Yes _____ No _____
   If yes, who conducts this inspection (title)? _____
   _____ And how often?_____

8. How are accident records and accident summaries kept? How often are they
   reported?

	No	Yes	Monthly	Annually
Accidents totaled for all company	_____	_____	_____	_____
Accidents totaled by project	_____	_____	_____	_____
Subtotaled by superintendent	_____	_____	_____	_____
Subtotaled by foreman	_____	_____	_____	_____

9. How are the costs of individual accidents kept? How often are they reported?

	No	Yes	Monthly	Annually
Costs totaled for all company	_____	_____	_____	_____
Costs totaled by project	_____	_____	_____	_____
Subtotaled by superintendent	_____	_____	_____	_____
Subtotaled by foreman	_____	_____	_____	_____

10. List key personnel planned for this project. Please list names, expected positions,
    and safety performance on last three projects worked on.

11. Do you have a written safety program? Yes _____ No _____

12. Do you have an orientation program for new hires? Yes _____ No _____
    If yes, does this include instruction on the following?

	Yes	No
a. Head protection	_____	_____
b. Eye protection	_____	_____
c. Hearing protection	_____	_____
d. Respiratory protection	_____	_____
e. Safety belts and lifeline	_____	_____
f. Scaffolding	_____	_____
g. Perimeter guarding	_____	_____
h. Housekeeping	_____	_____
i. Fire protection	_____	_____
j. First aid facilities	_____	_____
k. Emergency procedures	_____	_____
l. Toxic substances	_____	_____
m. Trenching and excavation	_____	_____
n. Signs, barricades, flagging	_____	_____
o. Electrical safety	_____	_____
p. Rigging and crane safety	_____	_____

13. Do you have a training program for newly hired or promoted foremen?
    No _____ Yes _____
    If yes, does it include instruction on the following?

	Yes	No
a. Safe work practices	_____	_____
b. Safety supervision	_____	_____
c. Toolbox meetings	_____	_____
d. Emergency procedures	_____	_____
e. First aid procedures	_____	_____
f. Accident investigation	_____	_____

(Continued)

g. Fire protection and prevention   _____   _____
h. New-worker orientation   _____   _____

14. Do you hold craft toolbox safety meetings? Yes _____ No _____
    How often? Weekly _____ Biweekly _____ Monthly _____
    Less often, as needed _____

SOURCE: Adapted from Levitt et al., 1981.

B

Guidelines for Using Contractor Safety Evaluation Questionnaire

Selection of the safer contractor can save your company money. Every year unsafe contractors are costing owners large sums of money for delays caused by accidents, possible third-party liability suits, and other direct and indirect resultants of poor safety performance.

The selection procedure described here permits owners to choose contractors whose past safety records are outstanding. Such contractors have developed outstanding safety programs already. High safety performance and its resultant savings for the contractor and the owner are already a regular part of their approach to construction. The owner not only is gaining a better total value from such a contractor, he is also reducing his own needs to monitor such a contractor.

The system is designed to be used for both prequalification for lump sum bidding and to help decide on which contractor to select in negotiated work. In situations for which selection is not possible, the owner can still use this system to indicate how much time and effort will be needed to monitor the particular contractor decided upon.

The selection procedure which is described in this document is easy to follow and use.

Evaluation Procedures

The qualification form items for safety selection in Appendix A are divided into three areas: contractor comparative safety record, management safety accountability, and formal safety program. The answers of each contractor to items in each of these areas will be scored and then summed to achieve an overall safety score for each contrac-

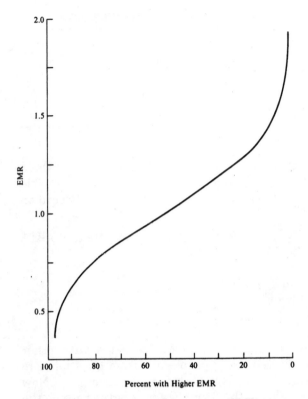

Figure B.1 Experience modification rate (EMR) versus percent with higher EMR (SOURCE: *Sample from California Rating Bureau, 1978.*)

tor. These safety performance scores can then be used for comparison between prospective contractors, or the owner can set a cutoff point to prequalify contractors.

Comparative safety record

1. **Experience Modification Rating (question 1).**   Using the EMR for the most recent year, which is given in Question 1, look up in Figure B.1 to find the percentile into which the contractor's EMR falls. After the percentile has been found determine the number of points to be awarded the contractor from Table B.1 and record on the tally sheet.

TABLE B.1   Points to Be Awarded to Contractor for Percentile EMR Position

Percentile	Points	Percentile	Points
100–90	20	50–40	0
90–80	16	40–30	−4
80–70	12	30–20	−8
70–60	8	20–10	−12
60–50	4	10–0	−16

2. EMR trend. For question 1, if the EMR is decreasing over the 3 years, give 4 points. If it is unchanged or there is no distinguishable trend, give 0 points, and if it is increasing give, 4 points. Record on tally sheet.

3. OSHA incidence rate. Using questions 2 and 3 compute the OSHA incidence rate using the following formula:

$$\frac{\text{Question 2 (a, b, c, and d)} \times 200,000}{\text{(Total injuries and illnesses)}} = \underline{\hspace{2cm}}$$
$$\text{Employee hours worked (question 3)}$$

To find how a contractor compares on incidence rates with other contractors in similar work, use the type of work from question 4 to select the appropriate chart (Figure B.2) for this type of company. Now compare the computed value from the formula above with those on the chart and find the percent of contractors with higher incident rates. Now use Table B.2 to find the number of points to be given to the contractor. Enter this on the tally sheet.

Management safety accountability

1. Question 5 should be scored as follows:
   Field superintendent   No, −2   Monthly, 2   Annually, −1
   Vice pres. of const.   No, −2   Monthly, 2   Annually, −1
   President of company   No, −2   Monthly, 2   Annually, −1
2. Question 6 should be scored as follows:

Response	Points
No	−2
Less often as needed	0
Monthly	3
Biweekly	4
Weekly	5

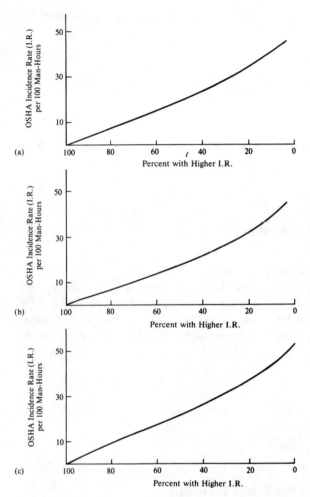

B.2 OSHA incidence rate (I.R.) versus percent with higher I.R. (*a*) nonresidential building, (*b*) heavy (non-highway) construction, and (*c*) plumbing heating, and air conditioning.

TABLE B.2   Points to Be Awarded to Contractor for Percentile Position

Percentile	Points	Percentile	Points
100–90	10	50–40	0
90–80	8	40–30	−2
80–70	6	30–20	−4
70–60	4	20–10	−6
60–50	2	10–0	−8

3. Question 7 (Do you conduct project safety inspections?) should be scored as follows:

Person	*Points*
No	−2
Yes, safety personnel	2
Yes, production and safety person	5

4. For questions 8 and 9 use same scoring system as for question 5 as follows:
   −2 for each No
   −1 for each Annually
   2 for each Monthly
   2 for both Monthly and Annually

5. Evaluation of roject personnel, question 10. The key field managers of your project are very important for controlling safety. An evaluation of their safety records on the last three projects they have managed should be made. OSHA incidence rates (see questions 2 and 3) are good means for predicting safety performance on your project.

Formal safety program

1. Question 11: Yes, 1; No, 0

2. Question 12: No, 0
   Yes but check less than 7 items, 1
   Yes and checks 7 or more items, 2

3. Question 13: No, 0
   Yes and less than 3 items, 2
   Yes and 3 to 6 items, 3
   Yes and 6 to 8 items, 4

4. Question 14: No, 0
   Yes and less often as needed, 0
   Yes and monthly, 1
   Yes and biweekly, 2
   Yes and weekly, 3

TALLY SHEET

Industry safety record
    a. Experience modification rating   _____
    b. EMR trend   _____
    c. OSHA incidence rate   _____

Management safety accountability
    a. Question 5   _____
    b. Question 6   _____
    c. Question 7   _____
    d. Question 8   _____
    e. Question 9   _____

Formal safety program
    a. Question 11   _____
    b. Question 12   _____
    c. Question 13   _____
    d. Question 14   _____
                        Total points   _____

* SOURCE: Adapted from Levitt et al., 1981.

References

Borcherding, John, Scott Sebastian, and Nancy M. Samelson: "Improving Motivation and Productivity on Large Projects," *Journal of the Construction Division*, ASCE, vol. 106, no. 1, March 1980.

Bureau of Labor Statistics: *Occupational Injuries and Illnesses in the United States by Industry 1984*, Bulletin no. 2259, May 1986, U.S. Department of Labor.

Business Roundtable: "Improving Construction Safety Performance: The User's Role," *Construction Industry Cost Effectiveness Project Report A-3*, New York, NY, 1982.

Business Roundtable: "More Construction for the Money," *Summary Report of the Construction Industry Cost Effectiveness Project*, New York, NY, 1983.

Hinze, Jimmie: "The Effect of Middle Management on Safety in Construction," *Department of Civil Engineering Technical Report no. 209*, Stanford University, Stanford, CA, 1976.

Howsafe: Distributed by Building Knowledge Systems, Inc., Stanford, CA, 1986.

Koch, James, E.: "Liability and the Injured Worker in the Construction Process," *Department of Civil Engineering Technical Report no. 283*, Stanford University, Stanford, CA, 1984.

Levitt, Raymond E.: "The Effect of Top Management on Safety in Construction," *Department of Civil Engineering Technical Report no. 196*, Stanford University, Stanford, CA, 1975.

Levitt, Raymond E., Henry W. Parker, and Nancy M. Samelson: "Improving Construction Safety Performance: The User's Role," *Department of Civil Engineering Technical Report no. 260*, Stanford University, Stanford, CA, 1981, (rev. 1985).

Levitt, Raymond E., Henry W. Parker, and Nancy M. Samelson: "The Role of Owners in Reducing Construction Accident Costs," *PMI 1981 Proceedings*, Project Management Institute, Drexel Hill, PA.

Levitt, Raymond E., Nancy M. Samelson, Gregory Mummy, Jean Brexta, and Lloyd Waugh: "Evaluation of the Line Foreman Safety Training Course," *Department of Civil Engineering Technical Report no. 281*, Stanford University, Stanford, CA, 1984.

Levitt, Raymond E., Nancy M. Samelson, and Daniel Murphy: "Assessment of Contractor Use of the Stanford Accident Cost Accounting System," *Construction Engineering and Management Program Working Paper*, Stanford University, Stanford, CA, 1986.

Parker, Henry W. and Clarkson H. Oglesby, *Methods Improvement for Construction Managers*, McGraw-Hill Book Company, New York, 1972.

Peters, Thomas J. and Robert H. Waterman, Jr., *In Search of Excellence*, Harper & Row, New York, 1982.

Robinson, Michal R., "Accident Cost Accounting as a Means of Improving Construction Safety," *Department of Civil Engineering Technical Report no. 242*, Stanford University, Stanford, CA, 1979.

Root, Norman and Michael Hoefer: "The First Work Injury Data Available from New BLS Study," *Labor Monthly Review*, January 1979.

Safequal: Distributed by Building Knowledge Systems, Inc., Stanford, CA., 1986.

Samelson, Nancy M.: "The Effect of Foremen on Safety in Construction," *Department of Civil Engineering Technical Report no. 219*, Stanford University, Stanford, CA, 1977.

Samelson, Nancy M.: "Crew Factors in Safety Performance in Heavy Maintenance

Operations," *Department of Civil Engineering Technical Report no. 275*, Stanford University, Stanford, CA, 1983.

Samelson, Nancy M. and John Borcherding: "Motivating Foremen on Large Construction Projects," *Journal of the Construction Division*, ASCE, vol. 106, no. 1, March 1980.

Samelson, Nancy M. and Raymond E. Levitt: "Owners Guidelines for Selecting Safe Contractors," *Journal of the Construction Division*, ASCE, vol. 108, no. CO4, December 1982.

Samelson, Nancy M. and Sylvia Mauro: "Benefits of Safety Management in Construction," *Preprint 83-010*, American Society of Civil Engineers, May 1983.

Index

ABOUT THE AUTHORS

DR. RAYMOND E. LEVITT is an associate professor of civil engineering at Stanford University. He earned his Ph.D. at Stanford, where his doctoral dissertation involved a study of how top managers of construction firms could reduce accidents on company projects. He was the principal investigator of the Business Roundtable study on the user's role in construction safety, completed in 1981. He has published articles and conducted short courses on safety management and developed a series of computer programs which evaluate contractor safety performance.

DR. NANCY M. SAMELSON, a social psychologist specializing in research on construction safety, is a safety management consultant to construction contractors and buyers. She is a member of the Safety Task Force of the Construction Industry Institute, a member of the Committee on Environmental and Social Concerns of the American Society of Civil Engineers, and a member of the Construction Division of the American Society of Safety Engineers. From 1971 to 1985, as a senior research associate at Stanford University, she spearheaded research in the area of human factors in construction management.